CANADIAN DOLLARS & SENSE

Buying Your First Home

IN THIS BOOK

- Buy your dream home!
- Discover who pays your Realtor (usually it's not you!)
- Find the folks who are more than happy to loan you money
- Get information about tax breaks and benefits

WILEY

John Wiley & Sons Canada, Ltd.

Library and Archives Canada Cataloguing in Publication Data

Buying your first home.
(Canadian dollars & sense)

ISBN 978-1-11-801367-0

1. House buying—Canada.   I. Series: Canadian dollars & sense

HD1379.B89 2010   643'.120971   C2010-906517-4

This publication is designed to provide accurate and authoritative information in regard to the subject matter covered. It is sold on the understanding that the Publisher is not engaged in rendering professional services. If professional advice or other expert assistance is required, the services of a competent professional should be sought.

Production Credits
Cover design: Ian Koo and Adrian So
Interior design and typesetting: Adrian So and Natalia Burobina
Cover image: © Thinkstock/iStockphoto
Printer: Printcrafters

John Wiley & Sons Canada, Ltd.
6045 Freemont Blvd.
Mississauga, Ontario
L5R 4J3

Printed in Canada

1 2 3 4 5 PC 15 14 13 12 11

table of contents

introduction

Buying a home can be one of the most joyful experiences of your life. But because it can be so complicated — and probably the most expensive purchase you'll ever make — it is generally also fraught with anxiety. One of the first decisions you need to make is whether you should even buy a home now. But assuming that you decide to buy, you not only have to be able to find the right home in the right location and for the right amount of money, you also have to find the right mortgage. In today's financially complex world, there are many types of home mortgages, with varying interest rates and differing lengths of repayment, and qualifying for the type right for you is essential. Only after you successfully navigate through the financial and legal mazes, go through the tortures of moving in, and finally awake in your very own home will you know you've done the right thing.

Why Do You Need This Book?

Can you answer yes to any of these questions?

- Do you need to learn about buying your first home fast?
- Don't have time to read 500 pages on buying your first home?
- Do you need to discover the best ways of finding a home you can afford?
- Do you want to be able to find the best mortgage on the market?

If so, then this book is for you!

How to Use This Book

This book discusses key things you need to know to make informed decisions about buying a home. For quick and easy access to a particular topic, you can:

- Flip through the book, looking for your topic in the running heads.
- Look for your topic in the Table of Contents in the front of the book.
- Look at the In This Chapter list at the beginning of each chapter.
- Look for additional information in the Resource Centre or test your knowledge in the Final Review section, both sections at the back of the book.
- Or flip through the book until you find what you're looking for — we organized the book in a logical, task-oriented way.

CHAPTER 1

heads you buy, tails you don't: making the decision

IN THIS CHAPTER

- Feeling good about buying a home
- Investing your money in property
- Keeping your money (from rent and taxes)

Close your eyes and picture yourself in your very first home: feet up, relaxed, your favourite music playing on the stereo. You're beaming. You've paid all your bills this month — including your home mortgage — and you still have a bit left over. Truly, it doesn't get any better than this.

Home ownership is about that good feeling: the incredible satisfaction of being grounded, knowing that you have attained the dream. You not only have a roof over your head, but it's *your* roof. A great feeling, and an accomplishment to be proud of.

On the other hand, because it *is* your roof, when the rain starts pouring through, *you* have to dig into your bank account and come up with a way to pay for fixing it.

Of course, you don't just plunk down your money and buy a home. You have so much to consider and so much to learn. You probably did your homework before you bought your car or decided which university to attend. You learned as much as you could about the options, and you may have even sought the counsel of others.

Congratulations! You made your first good homeowner decision by buying this book. This book can help you make all the other decisions about buying your first home, and help guide you through the process.

All the Reasons to Buy a Home

One of the most difficult decisions you make in life is whether to be a homeowner. You can experience all the joys of home ownership, or you can continue to rent a house or apartment and let your landlord have all the worries (and the profit). The following sections present some potent reasons why you should buy a home.

A home is a great investment

Much like a lever enables you to move heavy objects, a relatively small amount of your own money (the down payment) enables you to gain a substantial asset (a home). You *leverage* your money by using a little to gain a lot. Say you buy a house or apartment for $200,000: If you pay $40,000 as a down payment and borrow the remainder (called the *principal*), your investment is $40,000 and your debt is $160,000 (plus interest). If, a year later, the price of the house *appreciates* (that is, increases) by 5 percent, the value of your house increases by $10,000 to $210,000.

The increase in the value of your house — the $10,000 — belongs to you. So your $40,000 investment is now worth $50,000. A 25 percent return on your investment is not bad for one year.

Real estate is such a good investment because you can leverage your money in property. Very few people pay the whole price of a property up front. Instead, they put down a portion (often 20 percent or less) and borrow the rest. The invested money is leveraged.

Of course the price of your house could go down (*depreciate*) by 5 percent, and your investment would be worth $30,000. But the loss is only on paper. You experience no actual loss unless you sell the house at the depreciated price.

Interest rates are low

The lower the mortgage rate, the more home your money buys.

The interest rate you pay on a home loan is quite low compared to interest on other types of loans. Rates are particularly low at this point in time, which makes buying a home considerably cheaper. (Think way back to the 1980s, when mortgage rates were in the low to mid-teens, and the 1970s, when rates were around 20 percent.) Rates nowadays are under 6 percent, with some mortgage programs offering rates below 3 percent.

You're not a victim of rent inflation

You know how much rent you're paying now. And you can pretty much guarantee that your rent will increase over the years. If, as in Table 1-1, you and your family pay $1,000 a month now and your rent increases 5 percent per year — certainly a reasonable figure — the amount you'll pay next year is $1,050. The year after that, you'll pay more than $1,100. In five years, your rent will be about $1,215 per month, and so on.

Table 1-1: Rent Inflation at 5% Per Year

Year	Yearly Increase	Rent
1	base rent year 1 rent	$1,000
2	×5% = year 2 rent	$1,050
3	×5% = year 3 rent	$1,102
4	×5% = year 4 rent	$1,157
5	×5% = year 5 rent	$1,215
10	×5% / year × 5 more years	$1,550

In contrast, by buying a home and getting a mortgage with a fixed interest rate, your payments will be the same amount each month for the term of the loan. Conventional mortgages in Canada (some restrictions apply for loans insured by the Canada Mortgage and Housing Corporation, or CMHC) are for varying terms: usually six months or one, two, three, four, five, or ten years. At the end of the term, the mortgage is renewed at whatever the current interest rate is. So obviously, your monthly payment can increase. But it can also decrease because the rates are linked to national economic indicators. (Chances are pretty slim that your rent payments will ever decrease.)

Timing Is Everything

The prices of houses, like any other commodity, are sometimes high and sometimes low. But unlike other commodities, when housing prices fall, they usually don't drop very much. Timing is good for the buyer when the prices have stayed about the same or haven't risen much recently. Prices are good for the seller when they escalate quickly.

CHAPTER 2

so you want to buy a home: how do you begin?

IN THIS CHAPTER

- Choosing the type of home you want
- Working with the professionals

So, you've made up your mind to buy your first home. Now you have the daunting tasks of figuring out what style of house you want, where you want it to be, and how much to spend on it. Then you must navigate your way through a tangled web of forms, legalese, and the inevitable complications. This chapter helps you choose a home and select a professional team.

Looking at Your Housing Options

What kind of home do you want to buy? Aside from location and price, you can choose from a number of options in structure and type of ownership.

Single-family homes

A patch of lawn, a white picket fence — this is the single-family home that most people think of. A single-family home often has three or four bedrooms, a family room, a living room, a dining room, a basement, a garage, a kitchen, and 2½ baths.

Most single-family homes are measured in square feet, a valuation that encompasses the area between the exterior walls. Keep in mind that the total *square footage* figure included on a house's spec sheet usually does not include the size of the unfinished portion of the basement, garage, or rooms like a sunroom or screened-in porch.

An average three-bedroom, 2½-bath home is likely to be around 2,000 square feet. Add one more bedroom, an eat-in kitchen, and another bathroom, and you're probably closer to 3,000 square feet.

Condominiums

A condominium, or *condo*, is not a type of building, but a form of ownership. (Buying a condo, co-op, or new townhouse is very different from buying a single-family house. See Chapter 4 for more about these options.)

When you buy a condo, you actually do not buy the structure you live in. You buy the space the unit occupies — the airspace and everything inside. You own everything in the interior space, everything in the rooms and on the walls. But you *alone* don't own the walls, roof, or floors. Along with the other owners in your condominium complex, you share ownership of all the structures and the land on which the entire condominium complex sits, and you pay dues to your condominium's homeowners association, a legal entity that makes decisions for the entire facility.

Cooperatives

Cooperatives, or *co-ops*, are very similar to condos in that you don't actually own your unit: You are part owner of the entire facility. With a co-op, you don't even own the inside of your unit, as you do with a condo. A corporation owns everything, and you own a number of *shares* in the corporation, with the number of shares based on the size of your unit in relation to the other suites in the co-op. In a sense, you're still a renter, except that you're also part owner of *everything* (all the apartments and other structures, and all the appliances and facilities). You have the rights of home ownership and you have real property to sell, (although technically you are buying and selling shares in the corporation that allow you to occupy the unit), you have all the tax advantages and you have part of the responsibility for upkeep and maintenance of the facility. You also have the legal right to occupy your unit and a voice in the administration of the facility. See Chapter 4 for more about buying a co-op.

Townhouses

Owning a townhouse is similar to owning a condo: You own the contents of the structure and share ownership of all the common areas surrounding your unit. You likewise pay dues to a homeowners association for maintenance and upkeep. (One exception to this is a *freehold townhouse*, which the homeowner owns exclusively, without any condo fees — or services.)

One possible difference between most townhouses and condos is that with a townhouse your ownership and title may also allow exclusive use of a yard or patio, as well as the shared ownership of all the walkways and common areas. As with a condo, you own separate title to only your unit, which also includes the interior of the unit.

A townhouse often has more than one floor (in densely populated areas, it may have three or four), with the bedrooms upstairs and the living space on the first or first two floors. Townhouses look very much like the old *row* or *attached* houses (these touch each other or actually share a common wall) in urban areas.

Multiple-family homes

You can help pay for the purchase of your home by buying a building with one or more separate apartments or units (either side by side, upstairs/downstairs, or a combination). You live in one unit and rent out the others. The rent you receive for the other unit(s) frequently pays for more than that unit's share of the mortgage. Therefore, your rental income partially or totally offsets the cost of your own residence.

Not all areas permit multiple-family housing. Local government determines *zoning*: the zoning will determine the size and use of buildings in a particular area. An area zoned R-1 permits residential zoning — no commercial enterprises allowed — and only *one* family is permitted to live in each house.

Buying a Home Is a Team Effort

Although it's possible to do everything you need to do to buy a home by yourself, buying is generally too complicated, especially for a first-time buyer. You need experienced professionals to get you through the intricacies of buying and to ensure that the sale happens in a timely manner. A typical home-buying team consists of the following people:

- A Realtor
- A lender/mortgage broker
- Home inspectors

- An insurance agent
- A lawyer or notary

Figure 2-1 shows the people involved in getting you into the home of your dreams.

Realtors

People generally think of a Realtor as a professional who represents them in buying (or selling) a home. In reality, the term *Realtor* is a registered trademark owned by the Canadian Real Estate Association (CREA), which represents some 96,000 real estate brokers/agents and salespeople in Canada; only members of CREA, who adhere to that organization's strict code of ethics, are allowed to use the Realtor designation.

Figure 2-1: A cycle of the people and processes involved in buying a home

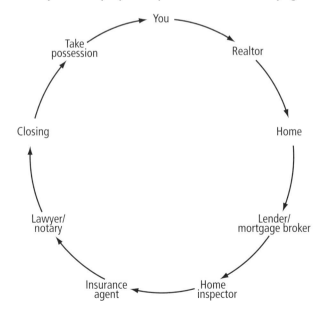

When referring to your Realtor, depending on where you live, you could be talking about:

- *A broker or brokerage*: A corporation or a person licensed to represent you in buying a home.
- A real estate *agent*: Like a broker, "agent" by definition refers to a registered corporation that employs real estate salespeople.
- A real estate *salesperson*, *representative*, or *associate*: This refers to an employee of a broker, brokerage, or agency who is usually licensed and who is given authority by the broker or agent to perform various services connected with real estate transactions within the guidelines outlined in the provincial legislation and regulations.

In this book, the terms *agent* and *Realtor* mean the same thing, except where noted.

Your Realtor or agent is the single most important person you deal with when you buy your first home. She helps you discover what you want in a home, shows you appropriate and available houses, helps you decide on the home you want, does the negotiating for you, refers you to all the appropriate professionals (inspectors, appraisers, and so on), helps you find the right mortgage (or helps you find the person who can), and guides you through the entire process. Finding the right Realtor is critical. Without this important member of your home buying team, you can easily get lost amid all the ins and outs of home buying. See Chapter 6 for more about real estate professionals.

Listing occurs when an agent contracts with a homeowner to find buyers for the seller's property. The listing contract is binding with the agent and with the seller. Your Realtor should show you all the houses that are available in your search area and price range. Although she may want you to buy one of the homes she is listing (that way she receives a commission as both the agent for the buyer [you], and as the listing agent for the seller) your Realtor should make sure that you are viewing every house that meets your needs. If this is not the case, you should get a new Realtor.

Realtor commissions can vary (from as low as 1 percent up to 6 percent) and may be negotiable if the agent you choose is prepared to negotiate their fees. Typically, the seller, per the listing agreement, pays all Realtor *commissions*. Be aware that commissions are included in the price of the house and are paid by the seller from the proceeds of the sale. However, you, the buyer, ultimately provide the money to pay them. Commissions are normally split between the seller's and buyer's brokers, and then by the brokers with their agent(s).

Lenders and mortgage brokers

Many people are willing to loan you thousands of dollars to buy a home. And not just banks, but private lenders as well, will jump at the chance to lend you large sums.

You must demonstrate to a lender that you're able to pay back the loan, and that the property you're purchasing is worth at least as much as you want to borrow.

The terms of a loan partly depend on the lender. So choosing the right lender makes a big difference in how much you pay for a loan. See Chapter 9 for more information on finding the right lender.

Mortgage brokers link lenders — including private ones — with individual borrowers. Lenders pay mortgage brokers a commission to find borrowers — in reality, the borrower pays the broker indirectly.

Why use a mortgage broker? Because you might end up paying less for a loan through a broker than you would by borrowing directly from a lender. Lenders, competing with each other, offer discount rates to mortgage brokers, who in turn offer discounted loans to you. The lender gets you as a client; you get a cheaper loan. The other advantage of a broker is that he will know of lenders you will want to deal with — lenders who might have less stringent guidelines for your financial circumstances for mortgage loans than, say, a bank or credit union.

Home inspectors

A professional *home inspector*, whom you hire, can tell you about the structure of the house, the foundation, the support beams and walls, the electrical system, the age and condition of the roof, and the status of the heating and cooling system. In older homes, you'll probably want the inspector to check for termites and other house-damaging pests, as well as for any building materials that might be hazardous to your health. The inspector reports to you any and all problems with the home and gives you a good idea of how long the furnace, appliances, and roof will last. Expect to pay $300 to $800 for the services of a home inspector, depending on the size of the house and the area of the country, and be sure the person you hire is licensed by the Canadian Home Inspectors Association or a provincial equivalent. See Chapter 7 for tips on how to hire a home inspector, and to review what an inspector should look at and for in your prospective home.

Hiring a home inspector is *essential* to your purchase.

You absolutely must know (and in fact, lenders might require that you know) whether there are any wood-boring insects in or around the house you are buying. An inspector can look for any infestations. Often, the seller is required to take care of insect infestations before the lender will provide the funds for you to buy the house.

Insurance companies

Every lender requires that you purchase property insurance so that if a catastrophe (such as a fire or flood) occurs, the lender won't lose their investment in the property.

Even if you buy the house without taking out a loan, you should have insurance. Property insurance rates are usually very low, although they can vary enormously. The rate is based on the replacement value of the home, and depends on the size of the house, the type of structure, and the location. (Rates vary by region and also by how close the house is to a fire hydrant.) Figure on spending about $300 to $1,000 per year, plus more for flood insurance if you live in a flood plain. The more your insurance protects, the higher your premium. Without insurance, you're responsible for the balance due on the loan if the house burns down or is destroyed by falling trees. Getting property insurance is a very simple procedure, usually requiring only a telephone call to an insurance agent.

For your first home, talk with several insurance agents to find out what the insurance covers and what it doesn't. Even though homeowner's insurance is a common product, and obtaining coverage takes very little time, a good agent is willing to spend time filling you in on what you need to know.

Lawyers

Although it's no more complex than other types of contract law, real estate law and transactions are affected by unique provincial and municipal regulations. And when it comes to closing your purchase and taking possession of your new home, you will be confronted with a confusing mountain of papers to sign and payments to make. For that reason, it's a good idea — if not a requirement — for you to hire a lawyer (or a notary, if you live in Quebec) to make sure your legal interests are being protected when buying a home.

In a real estate transaction, your lawyer will review the important documents you have to sign. If the buyer accepts your offer and you finalize your purchase, a lawyer will handle the closing arrangements.

A lawyer is a wise investment for first-time buyers. The protection you purchase can save you money and trouble. Be aware that fees vary widely — count on at least $500.

In the vast majority of purchases and sales, your agent will use standard forms, generally written and maintained by the provincial Real Estate Association. Be prepared for the fact that you might not get the opportunity to have your lawyer review all documents before you sign them. This is especially true in a hot real estate market, when time is of the essence.

Among the most important duties a lawyer will typically perform is finding out exactly what the property you want to buy consists of — not just physically, but legally. You need to find out not only how big the parcel of land is, where the boundaries are, and so on, but also whether the seller legally owns it and has the legal right to transfer that right of ownership to you.

If an up-to-date survey is not available for the home you wish to purchase, one option is title insurance, which protects you and your lender in the event of fraud, forgery, survey errors — all the things that might go wrong with the title to your property. Title insurance is often used when no survey is available. Your Realtor or lawyer can provide more information.

Usually, your lawyer will perform a title search on the property you wish to purchase, meaning he investigates the ownership history of the property. It's a check to ensure, among other things, that the seller actually owns the property you want to buy, and that it is free of liens, undisclosed easements, or other legal impediments to you taking legal possession.

Title, in real estate, refers to ownership. There are two main forms of ownership: "joint tenancy" and "tenancy in common" (Chapter 10 has the details). Your lawyer can help you make any decisions about the form in which you and/or your spouse/partner own the property.

You, and definitely your lender, should usually insist as a condition of purchase that the title to the property be clear of encumbrances. An *encumbrance* is anything that prevents a clear title, such as a lien, an easement, legal actions, unpaid taxes, and so on. A *lien* is an outstanding mortgage or other debt secured by a property. An *easement* is a legal grant to another person to limited use of land. For example, a piece of property may have an easement to allow utility lines to run through it, or an easement to allow use of a shared driveway. The easement will usually survive the sale and apply to the property when you own it, but you need to investigate any registrations and encumbrances on title before you finalize your decision to buy the property.

A *clear title* is a guarantee that your property is free of any liens except your own mortgage. You don't want to be surprised by undisclosed easements or liens on your new property, and, in the event that you default on your loan, the lender wants the right to *foreclose* — take and sell the property — to recoup the loan amount.

CHAPTER 3

what do you want in a home?

IN THIS CHAPTER

- Clarifying your needs and desires
- Finding the right place

Figuring out what kind, style, location, size, and price you want in your first home is easy: Sit down and think! Do a self-study!

Finding Your Dream Home: A Self-Study

Ask yourself the following questions, read the accompanying paragraphs, and check off each question when you have a clear answer:

- ☐ What kind of home do I see when I close my eyes?
- ☐ How long do I think I'll live in my home?
- ☐ How much do I think I can afford to pay for a home?

What do you see when you close your eyes?

Are you thinking about the home in which you grew up? Did your parents move to a bigger house as the family grew? Can you imagine yourself in a two- or three-bedroom home now but a larger one in 10 years when your income grows along with your family? What vision for a home does your spouse or partner have? Are your dreams the same?

Only you know what you really *need*. You can make do with less, or you can expand if you need more. Do you need four bedrooms? Do you need that second bathroom? Do you need, or will you need, a nursery? Do you need a playroom or a room for an office? What's the minimum you can live with? What's the ideal house and yard, or other type of home you want to live in? Where is it? You have to picture your family situation as it is now and how you anticipate it will be in the near future.

How much can you afford?

The amount you can comfortably afford to pay each month for your housing is figured by banks at between one-quarter and one-third of the gross amount you earn (32 percent for a mortgage, 40 percent for the total of all your recurring debts). If you earn $40,000 per year — about $3,300 per month — your housing expenses should cost no more than about $1,000 per month based on your salary, less if you have other significant debts (student loan payments, for example). If you have no debts and do not carry a monthly balance on your credit cards, you might be able to afford to pay a bit more. In equation format, it looks like the following:

Gross monthly salary ÷ 3 = Monthly housing amount
Example: $3,300 ÷ 3 = $1,100

But how does that translate into the cost of a home?

A simple formula for figuring an approximate amount for the house you can afford is to take the monthly amount you spend (or can afford to spend) for housing and multiply that by 200.

Monthly housing amount × 200 = Purchase price
Example: $1,100 × 200 = $220,000

You also need to figure in how much money you have for a down payment, how much you need for *closing costs* (see Chapter 10), and how much you need to put into the house immediately (including the cost of buying furniture).

How long will you live there?

Most people do not spend the rest of their lives in the first house they buy. Most people move every five to seven years. When determining the kind and price of the home you buy, give serious thought to how long you plan on living there. If you're a professional setting up a practice, or starting a new business, you'll probably stay a bit longer than the average homebuyer. If you're just getting out of school or you're in a job that you don't think you'll stay in for more than another few years, you may settle for a less-than-perfect home, planning for a better place the next time you buy.

Finding Your Dream Home: Where?

Do you like the hustle and bustle of the city? Do you like the convenience of walking down the street for a bite to eat, or for the movies, or for a cultural event? Or do you prefer life in a quiet suburb or rural area? You have to make lifestyle decisions when deciding what kind of house to buy. Here are five guidelines:

- The closer a home is to public transportation, the more it costs.
- The neighbourhood you choose has a significant effect on the price — and on your lifestyle. In many areas of this country people still do not lock their doors.
- The higher the unit in an apartment building, the higher the price (with the possible exception of the bottom floor in a small multi-family complex).
- The larger the homes in the neighbourhood, the more you have to pay even for a smaller home. (The most expensive home on the block is always more difficult to sell.)
- The closer you are to a school, the higher the price (unless you're on the same block).

Proximity to schools and services

You pay a premium to live in the area with the best public schools. Your Realtor may be able to give you information about the area, such as the number of local high school graduates who go on to university. You can also check out the Fraser Institute's Report Cards for School Performance, which score schools in much of B.C., Alberta, Ontario, New Brunswick, Quebec, and the Yukon (www.fraserinstitute.org/reportcards/schoolperformance/).

You should note how close the house is to the school and to shopping areas. Too far and the price is lower; too close and the price is also lower.

Your Realtor is not allowed to give you any information about race or socioeconomic class in a particular area. Realtors should not steer buyers from particular areas unless they have very good reasons. If you suspect your Realtor is guiding you toward or away from certain neighbourhoods without a good reason, you may want to consider finding a new agent.

Zoning is another factor in considering the location of a neighbourhood. Do you want to live in strictly residential zoning, in low-density zoning (for example, a minimum of one house per acre or four houses per acre), or are you willing to live in mixed residential and commercial zoning? If so, the price of houses will likely be lower unless it's right downtown in a city like Montreal or Toronto.

Proximity to shopping, parks, and public transportation, though desirable, also raises the price of a home. If you'll be commuting by train or bus, the additional expense may be worth it — probably not in actual dollars saved, but in the quality of your life and in the resale value of your house.

Proximity to work

Will you have to drive or commute an hour or more each way to work? Long commutes can seriously affect the quality of your life. Will your spouse or partner also have a longer commute? You may choose a home in the middle so that both partners commute the same distance. Unfortunately, in most urban areas in Canada, long commutes have become a way of life. To the extent that you can reduce the stress and anxiety of spending hours in a car or train, you can improve the quality of your life.

Don't forget that communities and highways change. You don't want to choose to live in a rural area only to find that a major thoroughfare is already on the drawing board. Your Realtor should be able to tell you the development plans for any area you're considering.

Orientation, view, and streetscapes

How pleasant the view is greatly affects the price of a house. This doesn't always hold true for some high-priced city apartments, but even in the city, a small two-bedroom apartment with a nice view may be priced much higher than a spacious three-bedroom apartment with only a view of the neighbouring building.

The placement of the house on the lot and the orientation of the rooms in the house also affect the price. For example, most people prefer that the master bedroom face the backyard for more privacy. How much light the house gets and whether the yard is suitable for a vegetable garden are other factors some buyers consider.

Likewise, the attractiveness of a home partly depends on the placement of the house relative to others. Is the house in a new development on a cul-de-sac (a circular dead end in which a few houses are clustered)? Or is it on a regular street with neighbours on either side and in back?

Traffic

Traffic partly determines the peace, safety, and convenience of your home as well as the resale price. Consider the following before you buy:

- How close is the house to a major thoroughfare?
- Can you get out of the driveway or turn onto the street during rush hour?
- Do people trying to avoid the busy streets nearby use the street as a drive-through?
- Are you allowed to park on the street overnight, and, if so, can you find a spot?
- Are kids who are playing outside safe from traffic?

Finding Your Dream Home: What Type of House?

You need to spend serious study time thinking about what kind of home you want. Some of the items discussed below may not be important to you, but they affect the price and you should at least consider them.

Style and structure

Your choices for the structure of a house are:

- **One storey:** Often called a *ranch-style*, *rancher*, or *rambler* house.
- **Two or more storeys:** The attic, whether finished or not, is the third storey — the basement is not included.
- **Split level:** Part one-storey, part multi-storey, in which different parts of the living space are on different levels. An example is shown in Figure 3-1.

Figure 3-1: A Split-Level House

Choosing the style of the home you want is one of the most important decisions you have to make, and one of the easiest, too. Eliminating the styles you don't want is usually easy. You have many styles to choose from, such as centre-hall Colonial, Victorian, Tudor, French provincial, Cape Cod, and the all-encompassing *contemporary* (a catchword for any style of home not covered by all the others).

You also need to take into account whether the house is wood-frame construction, brick, or some other construction. The style and structure of a house can have a major effect on the price.

Age

The enormous advantage of new homes (including one built specifically for you) is that everything works (or should). All the systems — plumbing, heating, air conditioning, electric service — should use energy efficiently and reliably. See Chapter 4 for more about the advantages and disadvantages of buying a new home.

A new home is generally considered to be one less than about five years old; historic homes are generally 70 or more years old. All other houses are, of course, somewhere in between. The age of the home can have a significant effect on the price. Be careful with historic homes: They may require a lot of repair and refurbishing, and older or more historically significant homes may be subject to certain municipal or provincial restrictions.

Condition

The condition of the house plays a major role in determining its price. The home's condition is also one of the areas over which you or your Realtor negotiates with the seller. When considering the purchase of your home, especially an older home, ask yourself:

- Are you handy with tools?
- Do you have time to spend making repairs?
- Are you even interested in handiwork?

Something goes wrong in *every* house, new or old. But then one of the best feelings you can have around a home is the sense of repairing or restoring it yourself.

Fixer-uppers, or handyman specials, as they are sometimes called in ads, are exactly what they sound like. You can get a wonderful, generally older home for considerable savings because of its rundown appearance. A fixer-upper may enable you to choose a great location, one of the key factors in the price of homes. Also, sometimes a house that lacks embellishments but is in good condition will sell for a lower price.

Any home is sold "as is." The seller of a fixer-upper is required to tell you what's wrong with the house to the extent that he knows, but isn't required to fix anything. Fixer-uppers can be excellent for people who have the expertise and interest in restoring or remodelling a home. But a fixer-upper can be a huge mistake for others. Fixer-uppers, like older homes, can be money pits.

If you're considering buying a fixer-upper, hire a professional to perform an extremely thorough inspection before you commit to purchasing the property. Watch out especially for homes that *look* good, but aren't.

Size of house and number of rooms

As a rule, the larger the house, the more expensive it is. Size refers not only to the house itself, measured in square feet, but also to the amount of land; that is, the size of the *lot.* In most urban and suburban areas, lots are measured by number of feet: 75 feet wide by 150 feet deep, for example. Also important is the number of *curb-feet*; that is, how much of your property touches a street.

In rural areas, lots are measured in acres: half-acre, 2-acre, 10-acre parcels, and so on. An acre measures 43,560 square feet.

A lot measuring, for example, 75 feet by 150 feet is about one-quarter of an acre. The area a house occupies on a lot is called its *footprint*.

Keep in mind that a corner lot often has no backyard and most of the land may be in front of the house. So the play area for young children on a corner lot has to be in the front; but be warned that many municipalities don't permit a fence around a front yard.

Regularly shaped and level land is more expensive than sloped, oddly shaped, or long and narrow land. When deciding between a house with a large amount of land, and a better house on less land, you may want to give preference to the latter.

The overall size of the house and number of rooms should feel natural to you. Are there enough rooms to accommodate your needs? Are the rooms tiny or adequate? Are the rooms so large that you have the feeling you stepped into a cavern and you can't imagine being able to furnish the entire house?

You grow to fill all the space available. So, in one sense, look for more space than you need. On the other hand, you don't want to pay for space you won't need.

Features and amenities

The more features, the higher the price of the home. And, of course, the more that can go wrong, especially in the case of pools, sophisticated electronics, built-in kitchen gadgets, and so on. Similarly, the more features, the more character the house has. Fireplaces are big price jumpers, as are eat-in kitchens, modernized kitchens — in fact, any nice kitchen. Pools, on the other hand, don't actually add much to the price of a house. A family with young children may, in fact, be very wary of buying a home with a pool.

The bottom line on features and amenities is that for every "cool" feature, you'll pay a premium. Then again, if you can afford it and you like the feature, go for it.

Bedrooms

Most houses are categorized by the number of bedrooms they include. Keep in mind that this number has a definite effect on the price of the home and on its resaleability.

Very few people want to buy a two-bedroom house unless they can have it for a very low price and then remodel and enlarge it. In some areas, even a three-bedroom home may not be attractive to many people — it's very easy to outgrow a house that size.

More and more houses feature a master bedroom suite — a large bedroom with an adjacent master bathroom and a dressing area that includes a walk-in closet. Even some older homes have been retrofitted to have this feature. A master bedroom suite can increase the price of a home dramatically.

Bathrooms

The number and size of the bathrooms is probably the second most important feature of a house. A master bathroom as part of a nice master suite definitely catches a homebuyer's attention.

In a three-bedroom home, you want at least 2 full baths. A four-bedroom home should have at least 3½ baths. (A *half-bath* has a toilet and sink, but no bathtub or shower stall.)

Bathrooms can be very expensive to install, so if you're thinking of buying a house that needs another bathroom or two, keep in mind that adding a nice bathroom can easily cost upwards of $25,000 or more.

Kitchen

This is it! This is the room that makes or breaks a sale. Even if you don't cook, you spend most of your time in the kitchen and adjacent area (there may be a family room attached). You may need to decide between a small kitchen area where only one, or at most two, people can work, and a kitchen where friends and family can gather at mealtimes. Do you want an eat-in kitchen (one large enough for a table), a kitchen with an island at which you can eat informally, or does it matter?

Do you plan to remodel the kitchen? Keep in mind that remodelling a kitchen is the single most expensive remodel you can take on: New kitchens cost a minimum of $25,000, and costs can easily rise to $70,000 or more. Not to mention that remodelling the kitchen is the most disruptive renovation you can take on.

When looking over the kitchen, note these important things:

- The amount of counter space for small appliances and meal preparation
- The amount of cupboard space for dishes, pots and pans, and food
- Whether the stove is gas or electric
- Whether there's a built-in oven or a range with a stove
- The size and potential traffic flow
- The lighting and airiness

Layout and flow

Layout and flow, also referred to as the *floor plan*, is an intangible quality in a house. Do you have to walk through the dining room to get to the living room? Is the room where you'll hang out or watch TV near the kitchen? Are all the bedrooms upstairs? If so, will that be a problem for your aging parent? Is there a powder room (or half bath) on the first floor, or will all your guests have to go upstairs when they visit? Imagine having a large number of people over. Will they be in each other's way or is there enough room? Does the house open onto a deck or patio? Is the patio easily accessible? Do you have to go through a laundry room or a bedroom to get to the backyard?

The flow and layout of a house is affected by the style of the house. Contemporary homes have unique layouts. You need to determine what's comfortable for you.

Garages: parking and storage

Most suburban and rural homes, including many townhouses and condos, have garages or some area for parking (such as a carport). Some are attached so that you can enter the house from inside the garage (thus eliminating wet groceries); others are a short distance away.

Some houses offer only street parking, which can be either easy to find or extremely difficult. Some neighbourhoods require a parking permit. Today, when many families own more than one car and need extra space for vehicles, more room for parking, especially protected parking, is an amenity that often means a higher price on the home.

Garages are used for so much more than storing cars: They also house workshops and workout areas, and allow room to store all the junk accumulated over the years.

There is absolutely no limit to the amount of storage space you need as you live in a home longer and longer.

Intangibles

Finally, you need to think about the intangible features of a home: Do you want built-in bookcases, a basement, attached garage, den, formal dining room, high ceilings, or central air conditioning? The key to deciding is to know what's available. How do you know whether high ceilings matter to you until you see them?

The best way to decide about features is to view as many homes as you can before settling on what you want. Make a list of all the features you absolutely love and those you detest. Then make sure you convey this information to your Realtor, to keep in mind when deciding on houses for you to view.

CHAPTER 4

condos, co-ops, and new homes

IN THIS CHAPTER

- Understanding different home types
- Examining the advantages and disadvantages of different home styles

While a mortgage lender may not care about the style of home you are buying, you care very much about what kind of home you buy, and you should know everything about your options. This chapter expands your understanding of three special types of homes and home ownership available, and what each type has to offer.

To review, you have a number of options when choosing the kind of home to buy:

- Single-family house
- Condo

- Co-op
- Townhouse
- Multiple-family house
- New house

Condominiums and co-ops require more specialized knowledge than regular houses: You may have to meet stringent resident requirements, and be approved by the board of the homeowners association before you can even buy a co-op. And if you're considering buying a brand new home, you have to deal with a builder or developer.

This chapter covers these three types of homes in detail.

Condos

When you buy a condo, you don't buy a building but a form of ownership. You own everything inside your apartment, but not the structure itself.

Along with all the other condo owners, you share ownership of the entire complex: the land on which the entire condominium complex sits and all of the structures. You are "part owner" of your unit, the common areas (the lobby of the building, the grounds, elevators, pools, tennis courts, gyms, and so on). As a result, you are partly responsible for the upkeep and maintenance of the entire facility — meaning you have to pony up a monthly maintenance fee on top of other housing costs (like a mortgage and property taxes) you might have. You have to pay dues to the condominium association, which has the responsibility of making decisions for the entire facility.

Advantages of condos

Buying a condo has several advantages:

- Condos are generally less expensive than single-family homes (although luxury condos are quite expensive).
- Condos include amenities, such as swimming pools and fitness rooms that you probably couldn't afford otherwise.
- The association has responsibility for maintaining the common areas, leaving you with very few maintenance chores.
- Problems that arise in the buildings are shared with the other owners.

Disadvantages of condos

On the other hand, buying a condo has some disadvantages:

- The resale value of a condo is generally not as good as that of a single-family home. (Note, however, that the continued growth of the population aged 55 and over is fuelling demand. In fact, in one recent survey conducted in several Canadian cities, 35 percent of the people polled said they were likely to buy a condo in the future.)
- You have less privacy because you share walls and common areas.
- You have little or no control over the maintenance fees you pay.
- Parking and storage space may be limited.
- You may have to adhere to strict noise, landscaping, and appearance requirements.

Condominiums spring from many sources, although increasingly they are fairly new structures. Therefore, overall, they are in better condition than older homes and apartments.

When you are thinking of buying a condo, in addition to the items you consider with a single-family home, you need to answer and check off the following specifics:

- ☐ How old is the condo complex?
- ☐ How many units are there?
- ☐ How many of the residents are renters and how many are owners?
- ☐ What is the turnover rate of the units? (A high turnover rate can mean that prices are depressed and that your investment may not increase.)
- ☐ What are the grounds like (swimming pool, fitness room, spa, and so on)?
- ☐ How smoothly does the condominium association run?
- ☐ What improvements does the association plan?
- ☐ How much money is in the condo's reserve fund to pay for those improvements, or for unexpected expenses such as pool repairs, or higher-than-usual snow ploughing costs?
- ☐ What are the restrictions in the covenants and rules of the condo association?

When you are thinking of buying a condo, you not only have to look carefully at the particular unit, you must also inspect the common areas.

Co-ops

Co-ops, or cooperative apartments, are very much like condos in that you don't actually own your unit. Rather, you are part owner of the entire facility. One major difference is that when you buy a condo you own the inside of your unit, and with a co-op you don't own even that. Everything — the walls and floors of every apartment, the lobby, the elevators, furnaces, water heaters, pools, gyms, and so on — is owned in common among the other residents, and you own a number of shares of the cooperative (which owns the building) relative to the size of your unit. You have the rights of home ownership and have the legal right to occupy your unit, and you have a voice in the administration of the facility.

Most co-ops are apartments, often in large buildings located in urban areas, and like some of the older condos, are converted rental apartments. Tenants at the time of conversion are often given the opportunity to buy their unit at a reduced price.

Advantages of co-ops

The advantages of owning a co-op are similar to those of owning a condo:

- You have a share in all the co-op's facilities, which means that you may have more amenities than you could otherwise afford and fewer maintenance responsibilities than with a detached house.
- Co-ops, like condos, are generally less expensive than comparable single-family homes because they have no yard or land.
- As a shareholder, you have the opportunity to participate in the running of the corporation, and thereby a greater say in who lives there, what services the corporation provides, and what expenses the shareholders must pay for.

Disadvantages of co-ops

Some of the disadvantages of co-op ownership include:

- You have to be approved by the board of directors of the co-op, not just by your lender and seller. Otherwise-eligible buyers may not be approved because of lifestyle issues unrelated to creditworthiness — naturally, co-op boards cannot discriminate based on race, religion, sexual preference, and so on.

- Some co-op boards require a down payment considerably larger than the amount lenders require — 35 percent of the purchase price, or even more.
- Because the deed to the property is not owned by any single person, getting a mortgage from a bank to buy into a co-op is difficult; some banks will not finance a co-op at all, and other banks may not provide traditional first-home financing for co-op purchases unless you have at least 35 percent down. (Credit unions might finance a co-op for less, but usually not lower than 25 percent down.)
- Selling a co-op may be considerably more difficult than selling any other type of home, not only because the entire board must approve of the buyer and buyers must go through the same approval process you did, but also because of the difficulty first-time buyers might have in arranging financing.

When you consider buying into a co-op, be sure you know, in advance, what hoops you have to jump through to get approved. And be certain you read and understand the articles of incorporation, bylaws, occupancy agreements, and financial statements.

Brand New Homes

There are three kinds of brand new homes:

- A home you build yourself, either with your own hands, or by hiring or serving as the general contractor for the construction.
- A home designed by an architect specifically for you (naturally with a great deal of input by you), built under the supervision of the general contractor you hire, on land you purchase.

- A home designed and built as part of a development from which you choose your location, model, and options.

You build it yourself

To build your own home, you must be very experienced in carpentry, electrical work, plumbing, and structural engineering, and have a strong knowledge of general contracting.

In addition, you must be sure you know exactly what you want in a home. Remodelling a kitchen puts a severe strain on your lifestyle and relationships. Building a home from scratch is even more problematic.

You hire a general contractor

Having your home designed specifically for you, geared to your needs and wishes, gives you an amazing amount of control and satisfaction. But it is not for the faint of heart.

Getting your perfect new home — with the multitude of decisions you have to make — is stressful.

You must make sure the general contractor does the job right. Delays, last-minute changes, and cost overruns strain your psyche as well as your wallet.

What you get is the house you want. You also get a house with the latest amenities and one that strictly adheres to building codes.

When you assume responsibility for overseeing the general contractor, you must take a very active part in the building process.

Make sure you:

☐ Hire a general contractor whom you know you can respect and trust.

- ☐ Understand all the conditions related to construction financing.
- ☐ Inspect the work at every major step.
- ☐ Be the one to make all major decisions about workmanship, style, and materials.
- ☐ Make certain that the contractors and subcontractors do exactly as the architect intended (unless you and the contractor have made changes).
- ☐ Keep a strict accounting of money paid and work done. (Always hold back a substantial portion of the fee so that you have some bargaining power if there are disagreements.)

You buy from a developer

When you buy a home from an established builder, the house is often part of a development, one of a handful of models designed for the area. While you can choose the specific builder you want, often that builder has worked with that developer before and has been approved by the developer.

Advantages of brand new homes

Buying a home in a new development has several advantages:

- You get to choose the exact house you want, and the amenities you want.
- Everything is new, which means that it should all work perfectly (and if it doesn't, you have a warranty).
- Because everything is new, you can be confident about the reliability of the major mechanical systems — electrical, plumbing, and heating.

- You won't have to do major work on the house for a while (replace the roof, paint the exterior).
- The house is the most up to date available, with enough electrical outlets, phone and cable jacks, and so on to handle the latest technology.
- New developments often offer recreational facilities for the neighbourhood.
- You can oversee the building process.

Disadvantages of brand new homes

Several disadvantages attached to buying a new home in an emerging development:

- Prices of new homes are frequently more expensive than comparable older homes.
- You have less room to negotiate the price.
- You have to be very specific about what you want, because many items are considered extras for which you pay more.
- Your choice of floor plan is limited to those offered by the builder for that development.
- The most desirable locations usually get developed first, so if you buy in a more established development, you may not get the best location.
- You may have to choose the house you want among professionally decorated and furnished models, and your home will not have quite the same look.
- The landscaping may not be complete when you move in.
- The house may look like all the neighbouring houses (or every fourth house).

- You might end up living in a construction zone for months, or even years, as the rest of the area is developed.
- The new home will be subject to GST and/or HST.

Just because a house is new doesn't mean it has no flaws or that it is well built.

Inspect the house during the construction process and before you take ownership. Make sure you thoroughly check out the builder's references and reputation before buying. If possible, look at other houses or developments put up by the same builder.

CHAPTER 5

how much can you afford?

IN THIS CHAPTER

- Understanding your credit rating
- Making a down payment
- Borrowing the money

When you finally find the home you want, your strongest reaction (aside from relief) may well be one of terror. You may ask yourself, "How in the world am I going to be able to pay for this?"

Sit down with your Realtor, maybe even your mortgage broker or banker, and crunch your numbers, and you'll likely discover that you needn't worry: You can afford it. This chapter covers figuring out just how much you can afford to pay for your home.

Would You Lend Money to This Person?

Unless you're independently wealthy, you'll probably need to borrow money to buy your home. Understanding credit and what lenders look for in a borrower is important to making your home-buying experience successful. Lenders consider your creditworthiness before they approve your loan.

Creditworthiness

Creditworthiness is determined by your credit history, which is maintained by credit bureaus. You can obtain your credit history from two nationally recognized credit bureaus: Equifax Canada (www.equifax.ca) and Trans Union Canada (tuc.ca).

Before you even start your search for a home to buy, you need to make sure that there's nothing in your financial past to prevent a lender from loaning you money for your mortgage. You can check your credit history by contacting one of the credit bureaus mentioned above (also the Resource Centre at the back of the book).

You have a right to a free mailed copy of your credit report once a year. If time is of the essence, you can view your report instantly online, but it will cost you $15. You'll pay $24 for access to your credit score — the three-digit number that tells lenders whether to loan you cash or not. Your credit score ranges between 300 (your bills line the kitty litter tray) to 900 (you borrow often, pay your bills on time, and don't carry a hefty balance on your credit cards).

If you haven't checked your credit history before, you should do so, if for no other reason than to ensure that your records are accurate and up-to-date. Errors and inconsistencies can occur, particularly if your name or address has changed. Be sure to resolve any problems as soon as you identify them so they don't interfere with your ability to qualify for a loan.

Good credit

Lenders require that you have a satisfactory credit history for a minimum of two years. A *satisfactory credit history* is defined as making continuous and prompt payments on all credit obligations, such as credit cards, personal loans, auto loans, and education loans.

Lenders may be unwilling to offer you a mortgage if you have any of the following in your financial past:

- Within five years: Defaulted loans
- Within seven years: Foreclosure, repossession, open judgment or suit, unpaid tax lien, education loan defaults, or other negative public record items
- Within 10 years: Bankruptcy

If you are self-employed, you must have been in business for at least one full year before filing a loan application, or have other, verifiable sources of income.

In general, if you are self-employed or get most of your income from sales commissions, most lenders will want at least three years of tax statements from you as proof of income.

No credit

Lenders are very wary of giving money to anyone about whom they know nothing. And, just as a history of defaulting on a loan will probably prevent you from qualifying for a loan, so will not having any credit history.

If you were lucky enough to have escaped borrowing for your education, have never bothered to get a credit card, or never borrowed to make any purchase, there's a good chance you will not be able to convince a lender to give you a mortgage. Ironic, huh? Here you try to be responsible by not borrowing and it ends up hurting you.

If you have no credit history, the first thing to do is to get a credit card and use it, making payments on time every month.

The Down Payment

Very few people can afford to pay the entire cost of a home all at once. Instead, most homebuyers pay a portion of the total price up front, and pay the remainder over time. The proportion you pay from your own funds is called the *down payment*. The rest of the sale price, which you borrow, is the *mortgage*.

How much down do I pay?

Your down payment is generally 5 to 25 percent of the total cost of the house. Although by law you can't buy a house with less than a 5 percent downpayment, some lenders may provide a portion of the 5 percent for you in the form of a cashback. Such arrangements are rare, and are probably not a good idea for most people. In fact, it's best to pay as much as you can down because the larger the down payment, the more favourable the terms you can get for your mortgage.

If you pay less than 20 percent down (not at all unusual for first-time homebuyers), the amount you are putting into the purchase is insufficient to cover the lender's exposure, so the lender requires that the mortgage be insured. Basically, if you default on your mortgage, the insurance pays off the lender. Typically, insurance for a high-ratio mortgage is obtained through the Canada Mortgage and Housing Corporation (CMHC), Canada's federal housing agency. Genworth (GE Mortgage Insurance Co.), a private company, also sells mortgage insurance. For a CMHC-approved mortgage, which is the most common, the premiums run anywhere from 0.5 percent to 6 percent of the amount you borrow from your lender, depending on the size and value of the home and on your employment picture. (Premiums are either added to your mortgage payments or paid in full when you close your home purchase.) That can add up. On the other hand, mortgage insurance lets you buy a home with a smaller down payment than is required for a conventional mortgage — as little as 5 percent of the purchase price, for first-time homebuyers.

For most houses, 20 percent of the sale price is a fairly hefty amount — a 20 percent down payment on a $200,000 house is $40,000. As a result, many people wind up paying for mortgage insurance — and the premiums can be costly. If you can come up with a way to prevent paying this extra fee, you're a lot better off.

Although the 5 percent down option is typically available only to first-time homebuyers, you qualify for it if you have not owned a home in at least five years, or if you had to sell your home because of divorce or job relocation. Of course, you can always get a CMHC-insured mortgage if you have more than 5 percent down, too.

Instead of borrowing more than 80 percent and paying for mortgage insurance, consider arranging a private loan or a second mortgage to bring your down payment up to 20 percent. So, in effect, you borrow more than 80 percent, but because of the second mortgage, you don't have to pay mortgage insurance.

This method has some qualifications and reservations:

- You must be able to qualify for the payments of the total amount you borrow.
- The second mortgage carries a higher interest rate than the primary mortgage.
- The second mortgage often is an interest-only loan — so for a set term, you pay only the interest on the amount owing. At the end of the term, unless you've paid more than the minimum amount, the principal owing is unchanged. The result: you've paid a whack of cash without building any equity in your home.
- The second mortgage is often an adjustable-rate mortgage, meaning that the interest rate fluctuates, and so does the amount you owe each month.
- The second mortgage may be due and payable within 5 or 10 years and is designed to cover you only during that initial period.
- Carefully weigh the additional legal costs, the current rates of interest, and repayment conditions associated with second mortgages to make sure that you are indeed saving money over paying mortgage insurance.

Where can I get a down payment?

You can get the money for your down payment from several sources:

- **Savings:** The most common source of cash for a down payment is savings. Many people stash away money specifically to buy a home.

  If you haven't done so already, start saving immediately for a house. The more you can save, the less you have to borrow (or, the more home you can buy).

- **Family:** A second common source of a down payment is from a family member. Many parents are willing to help out their children (if they are able) by either giving them a gift or tendering a loan. If you borrow from a family member for your down payment, you should have legal papers drawn up so that the source of the money is documented.

  If you borrow any funds for a down payment or for closing costs, the lender may look at that amount as a debt, and figure it into your credit score. Thus, it may reduce the amount you qualify to borrow.

- **Registered Retirement Savings Plans (RRSPs):** Under current Canadian tax laws, you are permitted to withdraw funds from your RRSP account with no penalty if you use the funds to purchase your first home. (The normal early-withdrawal penalty is 10 percent of the amount withdrawn.) You can use up to a maximum of $20,000 from your RRSP (and your spouse may also withdraw $20,000) to pay your down payment for your *first* home, but not any succeeding houses.

  Although your RRSP is an excellent source of funds for a down payment, you should also keep in mind that the true purpose of this money is to provide for you in your retirement.

  Although you can withdraw money from your RRSP to use as a down payment on your first home, the government also requires you to pay it back into your RRSP over a maximum of 15 years. For example, if you took out $15,000 of RRSP money to make a down payment, you would have to repay at least $1,000 a year into your RRSP account. If you fail to make the repayments, the amount that you don't pay each year counts as taxable income. So if you're going to take out RRSP money for your first home, be prepared to pay it back.

Table 5-1 shows the tax consequences of getting your down payment from various sources.

Table 5-1: Tax Consequences for Down Payment Sources

Source	Limit	Tax Liability
Family	None	None
Saving	None	None
RRSP	$20,000 per spouse (must be first home)	Must repay into RRSP over 15 years

It's All Up to the Lender

If you're renting an apartment or house, you know how much you can afford for your housing, because you know how much you have left at the end of the month. You know that you can afford to pay a little less than one-third of your total income for your housing expenses. Maybe you think you can pay even more for your own home.

Unfortunately, the amount *you* think you can afford really doesn't matter very much when you're buying a home. What really matters is how much a *lender* thinks you can afford. After all, it's the lender who controls the amount you can borrow. You only control the down payment.

There's a simple formula for estimating how much you can afford for a mortgage, plus all of your other housing expenses (property taxes, heat, etc.): Figure approximately 32 percent of your gross monthly income.

If your total income is $48,000 per year, your gross monthly family income is $4,000. Thirty-two percent of that is $1,280. That's how much a lender thinks you can afford to pay for your housing expenses per month.

Let's say taxes and heat cost you $200 a month. That leaves $1,080 for principal and interest on your mortgage, which translates into monthly payments for a loan of about $185,000 at 5 percent over 25 years (see the Resource Centre at the back of this book for websites with free amortization calculators). Assuming you contribute a down payment of 20 percent and borrow the rest, the $1,080 you can afford per month means you can afford to purchase a home costing about $230,000 including all lender's fees and other costs.

If $184,000 = 80 percent of the total, then 100 percent is $230,000.

But that's only part of the formula. Lenders also are concerned about your other debts because they have an impact on how much you can pay.

As a rule, lenders want all your monthly payments on debts to equal no more than 40 percent of your gross monthly income. This percentage is known as *total debt service ratio* (see Table 5-2).

Table 5-2: An Example of How to Calculate Debt-to-Income Ratio

Gross annual income:	=	$48,000
Gross monthly income:	=	$4,000
Multiplied by 40 percent:	=	$1,600
	=	Your total debt service ratio

This is the amount a lender feels you can afford to pay monthly for all your debt payments, including:

- Car loans (or leases)
- Student loans (yours and your spouse's)

• Credit card payments
• All other long-term debt

So if, every month, you pay $150 on your student loan, $250 for your car, and another $50 for your credit card purchases (which, by the way, you should pay off as soon as you can, because credit cards usually have the highest interest rates), the lender subtracts those amounts when determining how much to lend you.

Subtracting those required expenditures of $450 leaves a balance of $1,150 per month. This is the amount a lender believes you can afford to pay for your housing expenses.

Your mortgage payment is by no means your only housing expense. You also have to pay for homeowner's insurance and property taxes (figure approximately 2 percent of the home's purchase price), and in some cases condo or co-op fees, not to mention mortgage insurance if your down payment is less than 20 percent. Subtracting all these amounts further reduces what you can afford for housing.

Using the previous example once again, if you subtract insurance and property taxes — say $2,900 per year for property taxes and $500 for insurance, for a total of $3,400 per year, or about $285 per month — you now have just $865 per month available to pay for your mortgage:

$1,150 − $285 = $865

Using a mortgage amortization calculator, you can determine that $865 a month can pay for a 25-year mortgage of about $148,000 at 5 percent interest.

Add in a 20 percent down payment, and you can see that with an income of $48,000, you can comfortably buy a home costing just under $177,600.

hunting for your home

IN THIS CHAPTER

- Choosing a real estate agent
- Viewing prospective homes
- Buying directly from the owner
- Location, location, location

By now, you should have a pretty good idea of what you want in a home. Believe it or not, that was the easy part. Now comes the tough part: finding the right house. How do you go about it? Are there any shortcuts? Where do you get help? Right here! This chapter steers you in all the right directions.

Knowing Your Realtors

Real estate agents get their money from commissions, so if you never actually buy a house, they get nothing. Their primary motivation is to help you find a home to buy so that the deal moves to the settlement table. This is great for you because your agent will persist until you find a house. A good real estate agent does her best to make every transaction a good experience for everyone concerned — referrals are the way she builds her reputation and business.

But always keep in mind that a real estate agent will work for you but is employed by a licensed broker, not you.

There are three roles that a real estate agent can play:

- Seller's agent
- Buyer's agent
- Dual agent

When you're buying, you're not interested in an agent who represents the seller, but a buyer's agent. You need to make sure the Realtor you plan to work with does work with buyers on a regular basis.

The buyer's agent

A buyer's agent works on your behalf: He helps you find a home, negotiate the deal, and navigate through the entire process.

A buyer's agent may be paid indirectly by the seller from the proceeds of the sale. (The seller pays the listing agent or broker who then splits the commission with your agent.)

What's the danger to you? Say you instruct your agent to offer a very low price with the hope the seller will acquiesce, or at least come back to you with a counter-offer (*lowballing*; see Chapter 8). If you hire a buyer's agent, the agent is required to represent your interests, to negotiate with those interests in mind, and to keep your offer strategy and other financial information confidential.

A buyer's agent is often paid a percentage of the seller's agent's commission. As a result, even though you are the agent's client, you typically pay no direct fee for his services (although, obviously, he does get paid out of the money you give the seller for the house). Alternatively, you can set up an agreement (a buyer's agency agreement) with a buyer's agent to pay him from your own funds, whether or not you actually buy a house. Either way, his interest, responsibility, and loyalty legally belong to you. You can get more information about buyer's agents from the Canadian Real Estate Association.

The dual agent

A dual agent works for both the seller and the buyer for a specific property. A dual agent will be the listing agent or brokerage that is the one who signed a listing agreement with the seller, and also the one who agreed to represent you in the purchase of that particular house. You need to consent and agree to a dual agency arrangement in writing before your agent can act for the buyer and seller in a dual agency arrangement.

Like a buyer's agent, a Realtor working as dual agent will give you complete confidentiality under the terms of a "Limited Dual Agency" agreement. All information given by buyer-clients (you) and seller-clients will not be shared through the dual agent. In such a situation, a Realtor is obliged to honestly represent both buyer and seller and keep all confidential information absolutely confidential. But be careful.

If you look at or negotiate on any house listed by your agent (or any of the salespeople who work for the same broker/agent), she then becomes a dual agent and must disclose that fact to you in writing. Understandably, this can be an uncomfortable situation for all involved, and you need to be vigilant that your needs and concerns are addressed.

Finding the Right Agent for You

Working with a Realtor is the best way to find the right house.

How do you find the right agent? Usually one of two ways:

- Through personal relationships
- By doing research

In any event, you must do your homework to learn about potential agents.

Ask your family and friends

Like shopping for a doctor, lawyer, accountant, or hairstylist, the best way to find the right real estate agent is to ask friends and relatives for recommendations. And make it a point to ask your friends and relatives why they're recommending this agent.

The agent who helped your friends sell their house may not be the right one to help you buy your home. Learn as much as you can about the strengths and weaknesses of all the agents recommended to you so that you can narrow the list and get the right agent for you.

Scout "For Sale" signs

Check out the neighbourhoods you like and look at the names of the agencies and agents on the "For Sale" signs. Agents whose names appear frequently on signs are probably active in that community. Add those agents to your list of recommended and potential Realtors — an agent familiar with the area you want to live in is better equipped to help you find the right house. But remember that you're looking for someone to help you *buy* a house, not sell one. The expertise required is different for each process.

Go to open houses

Attending open houses (events at which houses on the market are available for viewing without appointment) is a great way to meet agents and to see houses. You can visit open houses in virtually every community on weekends — often between the hours of 1 p.m. and 5 p.m. To find open houses, look in the real estate section of local newspapers and local real-estate-related websites, or search out "Open House" signs as you go through neighbourhoods.

If you like the looks of an open house, walk right in. Meet the Realtor — who will likely not let you get past the front door without having you sign in — and explore.

Walk into a local brokerage

Walk into a local brokerage and ask to see a salesperson. But keep in mind that by doing so you're really relying on luck to find the right Realtor. If you use this method, make sure to ask the agent a number of questions, including:

- ❑ How long have you been in the business?
- ❑ Do you work with buyers
- ❑ Can you provide me with the names and numbers of some previous clients?

If you like the agent, great! If not, remember that you can walk away and find another one — even another agent in the same brokerage.

Search the Net

Scads of websites offer everything from finding you the right Realtor to securing your loan. *Don't believe them* — at least about finding a Realtor. Using the services of a Realtor means working with another human being and having that person work with you. Surfing the Net is no substitute for face-to-face interaction. But the Internet is handy for browsing through listings — in many cases you can even take a virtual tour through the homes' rooms. A website can't do much more than list the names of some local Realtors. You still have to meet and research them. Also, a photo, or a virtual tour of a house on a website shows you only specific views, and tells you very little about the neighbourhood, the condition of the interior, or any of a number of other essential elements.

You may be able to find good sources for financing your home on the Internet. See Chapter 5 for more information on financing.

Work with two or more agents

People often work with more than one Realtor, although doing so can sometimes get pretty confusing. Usually working with more than one Realtor means that you're looking in more than one area, and want agents familiar with each area.

There's nothing wrong with having two (or more) agents, particularly if you're looking for homes in a number of different areas. You should let your agent know that you will also be looking in another area at the same time — you may as well be upfront with the agent so that he knows you have other options if he or she cannot find you a home. The problem arises when the agents' areas overlap and you forget which house you saw with which agent. Also, if you sign an agreement with a buyer's agent, you may be liable for a fee whether that agent finds you a house or not; as well, your agency agreement might require that you use that agent exclusively for a certain period of time. As always, carefully read everything you sign.

If you work with more than one agent, be sure to keep good records of the houses you visit — including the name of the agent who showed you each one. Also make sure you tell each agent that you're working with more than one Realtor. But be prepared for the consequences. When agents find out that they're in competition for your business, they may drop you as a client or get you to sign a purchaser's agency agreement to ensure some kind of payoff for their work.

Except in very large areas, one good agent who really understands what you're looking for is more effective than several agents who just scour the listings for anything in your price range. A good agent always checks for new listings and shows you homes as they become available.

Meet with agents

There's no better technique than meeting someone to discover whether you get along. But even if you don't feel an affinity, don't rule an agent out. Set up meetings with all the agents you're considering. Explain to each that you're looking for a house in the area and are meeting with a few agents to choose one to work with. If any agent resists a meeting and wants to jump into looking at houses instead, tell her you'll call back (and head for the hills).

A good agent should:

- ❑ Ask what you are looking for in a home.
- ❑ Ask about your price range. An experienced agent can help you determine your price range based on your income and assets.
- ❑ Talk to you about getting pre-qualified for a mortgage and refer you to various lenders if you don't already have financing lined up.

❑ Explain how she will help you find the right home, including what she will do after you select a home, make an offer, and have it accepted. An agent should also tell you whether she can work with you as a buyer's agent or dual agent.

❑ Provide information about her experience and knowledge of the community, including how long she has been in practice and whether she works in real estate full time.

❑ Give you references of satisfied customers upon request.

❑ Introduce you to and have you meet with the broker.

Viewing the Listings

You and your agent have two ways to preview prospective homes without physically going to the home:

- The Multiple Listing Service (MLS)
- The Internet

Using the MLS — the Realtor's Bible

The Multiple Listing Service (MLS) is *the* essential source of information for finding your home. In most areas, a cooperative service of the Realtors puts together a computerized database — the MLS — which describes every house listed for sale by a Realtor. At this time, houses for sale by their owners do not get into the MLS, although this may change in the future. The MLS has different sections for single-family houses, condos, multiple-family houses, commercial buildings, and undeveloped land. Each section lists the houses in descending order of the asking price.

New MLS listings usually come out every day, and the database is updated continually. Each listing shows a picture of the house, the price, address, description (including number of rooms and their sizes), and some key information: whether an appointment is needed to show the house, whether there is a lock box, and so on. (A lock box contains a key to a house for sale and is accessible to licensed Realtors so that they can show the house to their clients at any time.)

Using the Internet

A second way through which you can preview prospective homes is by viewing listings on the Internet. The MLS online site at www.realtor.ca lists more than a million properties for sale. Your agent will often have access to a new listing a day or two before it shows up on the publicly-available websites. Homes that are for sale by owner are listed on other sites, such as forsalebyowner.ca. At these sites, you and your agent can search for listings by:

- Location — province, city, or postal code
- Type of home — single-family, townhouse, condo, and even mobile home
- Price
- Number of bedrooms and bathrooms
- Size — of home and/or lot
- General features — age of home, single- or multiple-storey
- Specific features — fireplace, family room, type of heat
- Exterior features — pool, size of garage
- Community amenities — proximity to transportation, golf courses, swimming pools, recreational facilities
- MLS identification number

To pick out the home you want, listings — either online or on paper — cannot replace viewing a home in person. To gain access to many of these homes, you must either go with your agent or make an appointment yourself by calling the listing Realtor.

Viewing Prospective Houses

Experience will teach you how to view a home efficiently. After just a few tours, you'll be able to take a quick glance at a place and know right away whether this is a keeper or a dog (and whether you even want to go beyond the entry).

How? Well, first, remember that you spent a fair amount of time defining what kind of home you want. You have a good idea about the kind and style of structure, the age, size, and features you want. You are pretty clear on the differences between what you want and what you need. You know how much you can afford, and what kind of neighbourhood you want to live in.

Given all this, you should be able to tell after just a few moments whether a house meets your criteria. And you fine-tune your standards as you look at houses, adding and subtracting features. For example, if, after viewing a few places, you realize that you absolutely can't stand townhouses, tell your Realtor so that he doesn't bother showing you any more of them.

On the other hand, keep yourself open to looking at as many styles of houses as possible. Just because you haven't liked any of the traditional, ranch-style bungalows you've seen doesn't mean you won't find one that feels right for you.

You or your agent can easily cancel an appointment to view a home.

Once you and your Realtor establish rapport, and you believe that he pretty well understands what you're looking for, you can relax a bit and trust his judgment. If you're considering buying a particular house, make sure you convey your thoughts to your Realtor.

The following tips can help you make the most of your viewing time:

- Consider the time you spend looking at the first few houses with your Realtor as nothing more than an opportunity for the agent and you to get to know each other. Be patient and realize that you both have some learning to do.
- Wear slip-on shoes if possible — you may need to take your shoes off at each home you tour. Don't wear those fancy new boots that lace up to your knees.
- Walk around the house with your Realtor and mention everything you like and dislike. Obviously, you can't be completely forthcoming if the owner or other potential homebuyers are around, but you can talk to your agent afterward.
- If you and your spouse or partner are viewing the house together, split up to save time. But one of you should stay with the Realtor to continue the dialogue.
- A good Realtor turns on all the lights in a house before showing it. To get a sense of what the house *really* looks like, turn some of those lights off.
- Take notes or take a brochure or information sheet if there is one. Especially if you're attending open houses, you see a number of houses within a short time span. It's hard to keep everything straight.

Use this checklist to help you evaluate specific houses:

❑ Evaluate the house's curb appeal. Take note of the impression you get of the house, and of the neighbourhood and other houses on the block. If you have strong feelings against the house, don't bother going in unless your Realtor has some reason for wanting you to see it.

❑ Walk through the common areas first. Take special note of the kitchen to determine whether the house is a possibility, and get a sense of the flow of traffic through the house. Look at the bedrooms and the rest of the house after you know the house has potential.

❑ Check out the house's orientation. Notice where the sun is in relation to the rooms and windows, where the house sits on the lot, and so on. Check the view from the major rooms, too.

❑ Open every door. That way, you discover whether there's enough closet space and see which rooms connect.

❑ Go into the garage and basement. Be sure to inspect the furnace room and basement bathroom (or half bath), if there is one.

❑ Notice the age of the major systems. These include the furnace, water heater, air-conditioning system, visible plumbing, and major appliances.

❑ View the deck, patio, or porch. Try to get a feel for what it will be like when you're sitting out there in the summer. This is a good opportunity to check out neighbouring properties and note the condition of the alley, if there is one.

❑ Take note of the amount of natural light the house gets. If you don't feel comfortable with the amount of natural light, consider the effect of adding windows and skylights, which is not prohibitively expensive.

Get to know the neighbourhood before you buy. Visit prospective houses at different times of the day, especially during rush hour and when schools let out, to gauge noise and activity levels. If possible, take a bike ride through the neighbourhood or go for an evening stroll. You can get a much better view either of these ways than you can from behind the wheel of a car. It can also help to visit the area's local police station. Ask whether there have been many break-ins in the area. What crimes are most commonly reported? How busy is the station?

Buying a House for Sale by the Owner

Some people decide to sell their house themselves to save the sales commission paid to a Realtor. Whether selling a house yourself is a good idea is debatable. Buying a house directly from the owner certainly makes the transaction considerably more difficult for you as the buyer.

The process of buying directly from the owner means that you're the one who has to find the lawyer, lender, inspector, and any specialists you need. Usually a lawyer or notary can help you with the process.

You find for-sale-by-owner houses by checking out forsalebyowner.ca or propertysold.ca, seeing a sign, reading about them in the newspaper, or learning about them from friends — they are not included in Realtors' MLS books or databases.

Unless your Realtor is a buyer's agent and you're paying him directly, he probably isn't interested in viewing a for-sale-by-owner house with you because he won't get a commission from the sale (remember, the commission usually comes from the seller). However, it may be worthwhile to have your agent ascertain whether the seller is willing to pay a commission to an agent who brings in a buyer. If the seller agrees, your agent can write the contract, arrange inspections, and facilitate the closing.

If the seller is not willing to pay a commission, you may decide to pay your agent yourself to help you seal the deal.

If you decide to buy a house directly from the owner, get a knowledgeable lawyer or notary to represent you.

When you buy a home directly from the owner, negotiating the purchase price is strictly up to you, with no intermediary. A house offered for sale by the owner is often priced a bit lower than comparable houses because the seller won't have to pay the commission.

Houses for sale by the owner are not necessarily less expensive. Owners may have no real knowledge about the real estate market, and often list their homes for what they hope to get for them. You need to learn as much as you can about what houses are selling for in that particular market. Or hire an agent to represent you.

Choosing the Right House for You

How do you decide on the right house? Chances are that you like more than one of the houses you've seen. So how do you choose?

Remember two things:

- You'll likely see a wide variety of different homes — comparing specific houses can be very difficult.
- There's no absolutely right or wrong choice for you.

How do you compare a three-bedroom Cape Cod-style house on a nice quarter-acre lot in the suburbs with a townhouse a short walk from the train station? You trade off things, and try to equate what you can.

Keep in mind that you live *inside* the house, not on the land. Generally, you're better off choosing a better house than better land. On the other hand, never forget the importance of "location, location, location." You can always improve the house. There's not much you can do about the location.

Ultimately your decision should be based on the following criteria:

- ❑ **The price:** Can you afford it?
- ❑ **The style and size of the house:** Does it suit your lifestyle and needs?
- ❑ **The location and proximity:** Is it close to where you need to be?
- ❑ **The condition of the house:** How much work does it need?
- ❑ **The intangibles:** Does it feel right?

CHAPTER 7

checking out the house you want

IN THIS CHAPTER

- Why you should inspect a house
- Who should inspect
- The inspection checklist

Don't Buy a House Sight Unseen

Your home is likely to be the most expensive purchase you make in your life (second only to your next home). Imagine buying a used car. Do you buy it without going over it thoroughly to make certain that it's in good condition? Not only do you look over everything, you probably have a mechanic go over it as well.

With a home, regardless of whether it is brand new, a few years old, or considered historic, you absolutely, positively *must* have it inspected. Most purchase agreements include a contingency or conditional clause specifying that you have a defined period of time for a home inspection before the deal is considered consummated. Buyers who waive this clause in a competitive seller's market do so at their own risk.

There are three different inspections you should make when buying your first home:

- Initial walk-through
- Second (repeat) viewing
- Professional inspection

Your initial walk-through

The first time you walk through a house is probably during the house-hunting stage when all you're doing is getting the feel of each house. (Review Chapter 6 to go over what to look for when you first walk through a home.)

Your second viewing

The second time you walk through a house you're more serious. You've narrowed down your selections to this particular house and maybe a few others. Now you're deciding whether or not to put in an offer. So before you do, you and your Realtor go back to the house for another walk-through. What do you do this time? You're there to really check out the house to see what condition it is in. You're considering not just the feel of the house, but whether your family will be happy there and, if so, what will have to be done to the house to make it what you want. Be sure to look over, and when appropriate, use the home inspection checklist later in this chapter.

Here are a few tips:

❑ Schedule the second viewing with your Realtor and make certain you and your spouse or partner can both go.

❑ If you have children, bring them, if they are old enough to be a part of the decision-making and if they won't be a distraction.

❑ To get a different perspective, consider viewing the house at a different time of day than when you last viewed it (night versus day). However, if your spouse or partner didn't see the house during the day, go again during the day because seeing the house in daylight is very important. You can always schedule a third visit for the evening hours.

❑ Ask that the sellers be there, if possible, although most selling agents prefer buyers and sellers not to meet before a deal is made. If the seller is there, you have a good opportunity to ask a few questions. By asking innocent and general questions (e.g., Does all the plumbing work?), you may find out a lot.

❑ Bring a tape measure to do quick measurements of the rooms and locations of the windows and doors. (The MLS listing and/or information sheet has the approximate room sizes, but you need to see whether your furniture will fit.)

❑ Flush the toilets and run the water (including the showers) to see whether they all work properly and to check the water pressure.

❑ Go through the closets to see how much storage space there is.

❑ Go down to the basement to see how old the furnace, hot-water heater, and circuit-breaker box are. (If there's a fuse box, you know you have to upgrade the wiring.)

❑ Pay special attention to the condition of the house, including the floors, walls, and ceilings. Look for cracks in the foundation, bowed walls and uneven or spongy floors — often signs of structural problems.

❑ Look for water spots, peeling wallpaper or paint, missing shingles, siding, or bricks, and other stains. Use your nose to detect signs of mould or mildew.

❑ Take careful notes about concerns, answers to questions, and questions that need to be addressed. Do a quick sketch of the floor plan if you can.

The Professional Inspection

Although you are not required to have an inspection by a licensed professional, it is strongly recommended. The cost for an inspection ranges from about $300 to $800, depending on the area and the size of the house. Even if your house is brand new and you are the first person to occupy it, you should still have the house inspected by a professional. You're spending thousands of dollars on probably the largest investment of your life — don't skimp on what is the most valuable evaluation of that investment.

The inspection is usually done within a week of signing the purchase agreement and is usually one of the conditions on which the sale is based. Be sure the inspector you hire is licensed by the Canadian Association of Home and Property Inspectors (cahpi.ca) or a provincial equivalent.

If the house does not pass inspection — there are things wrong that you believe will be too costly to repair or replace — you are perfectly within your rights to cancel the contract as long as the period in the clause of the purchase agreement has not expired.

The question you must answer is "Under what conditions, discovered in the home inspection, should I cancel the contract?"

The best answer is "none," unless you're having second thoughts about the house anyway. Why? Because an inspection that reveals major damage shouldn't close off all possibilities. Instead, it should open up a dialogue between you and the seller. However, if you are in a very hectic sellers' market, be prepared that the seller may be reluctant to renegotiate the terms of your offer. In an ideal scenario, your options are:

- If there is extensive damage and you want the house but don't want to pay for the repairs or replacement, negotiate to have the seller pay for them.
- If there is minor damage and you want the house, negotiate to have the work taken care of by the seller or to get a monetary credit (a reduction in price) for the repairs.
- If there is extensive damage and you don't want the house because of the problems, keep your options open and maybe the seller will make you an offer you can't refuse, but you should be very careful and be prepared to walk away.

If serious concerns arise in any one area, find out as much as you can from the sellers, and be sure to discuss the problems with a professional or two who have expertise in repairing that type of problem. For example, for structural problems, consult a structural engineer; for water leaks, a plumber, and so on. Take careful notes about the type and condition of each element so you know exactly what you are buying and any repair costs. You should also try to find out the age of the roof, heating and air conditioning systems, and all appliances. This gives you an idea about when you will have to replace them.

Follow the home inspector while she's doing the inspection. It's a real education in the condition of the house — and in what kind of maintenance and other expenses you can expect as a homeowner.

Structure

The inspector notes the type of foundation the house is built on (brick, concrete, wood, or stone) and its condition, and also checks the shape of the basement, crawl spaces, and the house's support system, which includes the framing, joists, and roof trusses and rafters.

Electrical

Make sure you know the location of the main breaker. Ask the sellers or your inspector to show you where it is. A professional inspection includes checking the following:

- Amps at power supply
- Condition of the wiring
- Electrical panel and condition of the breakers or fuses
- Location, number, and condition of outlets and switches (including whether the kitchen and bathrooms have ground fault interrupter circuits)
- Outside wiring and lighting
- Power line
- Switches and dimmers
- Type and location of grounding

Heating and air conditioning

Your inspector notes the type of heating and air conditioning systems and checks their condition and approximate age. Checking the condition includes inspecting the ducts and filters, the thermostats, and the safety features of a wood stove, if there is one.

Plumbing

You can test the quality and flow rate of the water by turning on all the taps. Your inspector also checks the water supply line and the main shutoff valve, the type and condition of interior plumbing, the age and condition of the water heater, and makes sure all faucets and toilets function and that all water drains properly.

Interior

Your inspector pays attention to the following (many of these items and conditions are obvious enough that you can form an opinion of their condition yourself):

- ❑ Alarms (smoke, heat, and carbon monoxide detectors)
- ❑ Attic ventilation
- ❑ Chimney and fireplace
- ❑ Doors and door jambs (including the garage door)
- ❑ Floors (including stairways and railings)
- ❑ Insulation
- ❑ Walls and ceilings
- ❑ Windows

Kitchen

In this room, too, you can follow along with your inspector:

- ❑ **Appliances:** Check the ease of operation of the oven, stove, exhaust fan, microwave, refrigerator, dishwasher, and garbage disposal if they are included in the sale.
- ❑ **Cabinets:** Do the doors open and close properly; are the shelves even and supported?
- ❑ **Countertops:** Check for scratches, burns, and stains, and find out whether the material is long-lasting and easy to clean.

❑ **Floors:** Check for loose, scratched, or damaged tiles or linoleum and for stained carpet.

❑ **Sinks and faucets:** Check the material they're made of (generally porcelain or steel); look for drips and stains; make sure that bathtubs and sinks are well caulked.

❑ **Ceilings:** Look at the surfaces above; check for stains and cracks.

Exterior

Your inspector notes the condition of the driveway, roof, chimney, gutters and downspout, and siding and trim. The inspector also makes sure that trees aren't damaging the foundation or siding, and that the slope of soil around the foundation encourages water to drain away from the house, not toward it.

Pest inspection

One of the benefits of Canada's northern climate is that home-damaging pests usually do not present a huge headache for homebuyers. On the other hand, termites, carpenter ants, and other wood-boring insects are an increasing concern in certain areas of the country, especially in parts of Toronto. If you are considering a home in an affected area, it's a good idea to check the qualifications of your home inspector to ensure she is experienced in pest inspection. Typically, an inspector will look for damage done by pests in the past so that you can be certain the house does not have any serious structural damage — the cost to repair such damage can be high.

In some areas, lenders may require a professional pest inspection because damage resulting from pests can be extensive and may shorten the life of the house. If the house deteriorates, the lender's equity (the investment they have in the house via the mortgage) would thus be jeopardized.

The cost of a pest inspection usually is included in the home inspector's fee. If termites or other pests show up, hire a pest control company to eliminate pest infestation. A contractor puts a large tarpaulin over the house (*tenting*) and sprays it. The house remains empty for a few days but then is quite safe to enter. The cost for tenting and spraying the house can run $1,000 or more; usually, a yearly fee in the neighbourhood of $300 to the pest control company acts as an insurance policy in case another infestation occurs.

Even if your lender does not require a pest inspection, it is strongly recommended that you have one done on any house you are buying, and consider making the sale contingent upon finding no evidence of infestation.

CHAPTER 8

the business of buying a home

IN THIS CHAPTER

- Determining how much to pay
- Negotiating the price you want
- Assessing what you get for your money

Finding the right house and figuring out the financing is tough. When you begin the business of buying a home, you face a maze of legalese and numbers. This chapter guides you through the process of putting in a bid to buy a house, responding to counter-offers from the seller, and negotiating the final price. You also find out how to make sure you know what it is you're buying.

Bidding on a House

Getting to a final sales price is like a game, but not a game for the timid. Everyone knows that the seller's asking price is just the first move — a starting point. And everyone expects some give and take until both the buyer and seller are comfortable with the final price. You can think of the seller's listing price as the real initial offer, her opening bid. From that bid, the negotiations begin.

Imagine that the seller is asking $229,000 for the home you want. You think that the house is priced pretty fairly in comparison to all the other houses you've seen, and your Realtor's comments indicate that he thinks the price is reasonable. But you surely don't want to pay the full listing price because the house has been on the market for more than a month in a *seller's market* (when there are more buyers than houses for sale), which indicates that the price may be too high.

How much do you offer?

You should consider several strategies:

- **Be reasonable:** Some professionals suggest that you make your first bid reasonable so that you don't insult the seller. (You may need the seller's goodwill later in the process.) A reasonable offer is an excellent strategy to use in a seller's market. The disadvantage is that you may end up paying a higher price than you would using a different strategy.

   In most instances, a *reasonable offer* is at least 90 percent of the asking price, although in some markets 95 percent is reasonable. In a very strong seller's market, the asking price, or a bit below, is an appropriate offer. Your Realtor can give you data about the asking price versus the selling price of homes in the particular area.

- **Lowball:** In a buyer's market (when there are more sellers than buyers), or if the house has been on the market for a long time, offering significantly less than the asking price may be acceptable if the seller is really anxious to sell the house. Offering $190,000 for a $229,000 asking price is an example of a lowball offer. See more on making lowball offers in the "Counter-offers and counter-counter-offers" section later in this chapter.

• **Round numbers:** Most houses are listed for prices ending with a four or a nine, to give the buyer the feeling that the price is less. This is a classic marketing manoeuvre, and though it doesn't really fool anyone, an asking price of $229,000 does sound less than $230,000. (While it is usually the best practice to use nines, in some instances it can actually hurt the seller. For example, with 229, you know the seller wants to stay in the 220s, and may even go as far down as 220. With an asking price of 230, there is the sense that there's less room for negotiating; that is, the seller would probably accept 225, but maybe not less than that. Of course, all offers depend on the market conditions.)

When you make an offer, use the number that sounds higher (230 sounds much higher than 229), so round numbers are generally preferred. Sometimes you see asking prices using complex numbers such as $224,599. The feeling conveyed here is that the process of determining that precise number was deliberate and tied into the exact amount the seller will accept. Don't get fooled. With numbers in the tens of thousands, a few hundred dollars in either direction are irrelevant.

Throughout the negotiating process, you need to rely on two things: doing your homework and having a Realtor you can trust.

Doing your homework

You absolutely must prepare before you make your initial offer to buy a home. Answer these questions:

- ☐ How much have comparable houses in the area sold for?
- ☐ How long were those houses on the market?
- ☐ What were their initial asking prices?
- ☐ Were those prices reduced at any time?
- ☐ What is the maximum price you can pay for this house and still feel comfortable?
- ☐ Are you willing to lose this house?
- ☐ How much of a hurry are you in to find a home?

Trusting your Realtor (and yourself)

Your Realtor is a professional who has likely been through negotiations many times over. There's a good chance that she knows the sellers' Realtor and she may have some insight into the seller's expectations from the seller's agent. Furthermore, your agent knows the market conditions and has a pretty good idea of a fair price for houses in the area. It's very unlikely — and would be highly unethical — that she will try to convince you to bid higher, hoping to receive a larger commission. (If you're arguing about three or four thousand dollars, the difference in each realtor's share of the commission is just $100 or $120, which is hardly worth her time to worry about.) More important, your potential referrals are much more beneficial to her than 100 bucks.

If you are strongly attached to buying a particular house, you don't want to lose the deal because of a small amount of money. In a strong seller's market, you can easily lose out to someone who offers more — maybe more than the asking price!

On the other hand, while trusting your Realtor's knowledge and expertise, unless she's acting for you as a buyer's agent under a buyer agency contract, you must also be very aware of who she works for: herself. She gets paid only when the sale goes through. So, although she will work very hard to ensure that your deal goes through, her main focus may be on getting to that end point, not necessarily on making sure that you spend the least amount of money to get there.

Although your agent must honour the information you give her in confidence, and use the knowledge she has of your situation to your benefit, think twice before you tell her:

- How much you are willing to pay for the house
- That you absolutely must have this house

Counter-offers and Counter-Counter-offers

In home-purchase negotiations, typically you make an offer and the seller comes back with a counter-offer — an amount a little less than the original asking price. Then you come up a bit, too. And the two of you may haggle like this for several rounds when you're negotiating amounts over thousands of dollars.

You have two goals in your offer and counter-offer strategy, which sometimes can be in conflict with each other:

- Buy the house for the lowest possible price the seller is willing to accept.
- Keep on the good side of the seller so you don't lose the deal later by quibbling over small things, such as closing dates or minor repairs that you want done.

Lowballing

Some sellers feel insulted and get very upset with a lowball offer, while other sellers take it in stride and either make a counter-offer or simply ignore your offer.

If you really want this home, do not lowball unless your Realtor has information indicating that your low offer won't be received negatively. If you annoy the sellers, they're likely not to accept even a reasonable offer from you later on.

How low is lowballing? It depends — there's no actual definition. You and your Realtor can determine what a lowball offer is by looking at the amount houses have sold for relative to the asking price. If houses routinely sell for 5 to 7 percent below the asking price, an offer 10 percent below that price is considered quite reasonable, and an offer 20 percent less than the asking price is considered a lowball offer. On the other hand, if houses have been selling for just 2 or 3 percent below asking, and sometimes above asking price, an offer of just 5 percent below asking price may be considered lowballing.

The MLS listing shows how long a house has been on the market, although occasionally a house is put on the market, then off for a while before being put back up for sale. Your Realtor should be able to give you information about the sales and listing history of the house you're interested in.

Take several factors into consideration when making a decision about lowballing a seller:

- How long the house has been on the market. If the house has been on the market for three months or more without an offer being accepted, the seller probably won't be surprised to see a lowball offer.

- The asking price is considerably higher than comparable homes in the area.
- Other elements of your offer are particularly strong. If you can make a large down payment (more than 25 percent), a large deposit, or can be flexible about closing on the home, a lowball offer may be more acceptable. (Some sellers are willing to take less for their house if, for example, the buyer can close within 30 days.)
- You're not very committed to this house. You may be willing to buy the home at a low price, but not be disappointed if you lost it.
- The area is experiencing a strong buyer's market. In this situation, often there are many other homes available at the price you're willing to pay.
- Your Realtor has particular knowledge of the seller's willingness to sell the property at a considerably lower price.

Conditions

Generally, when you make an offer, you build in conditions — sometimes called *contingencies* or "*subject to*" clauses — before the sale can go through. Contingencies usually include:

- Lawyer review — usually within three business days
- Obtaining a mortgage — usually three days to a week. (Few sellers are willing to tie up their property for longer than that.)
- Home inspection — usually within one week

You can use these time periods to consider all your options, renegotiate if appropriate (if something needs to be repaired, for example), and even to get out of the deal under certain conditions.

Getting What You Pay For

When you buy a home, you get title to property and receive a deed to that property. (*Title* and *deed* are legal terms covered in Chapter 10.) Other than the walls, floor, ceilings, and roof, what do you get when you purchase a home? When you buy a single-family, detached home, you also buy the land under the house (called the *footprint*), the airspace above the house, and the lot as defined in the deed. When you buy a condo, co-op, or townhouse, you may be owner of your unit and part owner of the common areas (see Chapter 2).

Be totally clear about what it is you are buying: Ask your Realtor or lawyer or notary to explain to you exactly what you're buying.

While you're still in the negotiating phase, be clear in your offer in writing about what stays with the house, what goes with the sellers, and whose responsibility it is if something goes wrong in the time before the home changes ownership. Some of the standards for these issues are spelled out in the *agreement of purchase and sale* (the contract between buyer and seller specifying the price and terms of sale).

Everything is negotiable, and you should make sure you understand what you are purchasing.

Fixtures and appliances

The general rule about appliances is that if they are not outlined and listed in a purchase offer, the vendor is taking them before you take possession of the house. However, light fixtures and heating and plumbing fixtures that are affixed to the property are generally included, unless the seller specifies in the contract that they would like to keep the dining room chandelier, for example.

Sellers generally do not have to replace any fixture they take with them unless the contract specifically requires them to replace the removed fixture with another one.

Plantings

Like fixtures, most trees and shrubs stay since it is difficult to take them. Unless the listing specifies, you can assume that all plantings stay. If a particular tree, shrub, or plant is to go with the seller, it should be so labelled (and specifically mentioned in the contract) and the seller should make sure that removing the plant doesn't leave a hole. The sellers are usually not obligated to replace the planting.

Holes and damage to walls

Behind most pictures and wall hangings are holes. Usually they are not repaired when the seller vacates, and most of the time they are tiny holes. Chances are that when you decorate, you'll use the same holes or, at least, cover them with your pictures. If a hole is particularly bad, you can hope that the seller repairs it before leaving — but don't count on it.

If you are concerned about damaged walls, carpet stains, broken windows, or other cosmetic damages, mention these in the contract rather than waiting for the final walk-through (see Chapter 7). Waiting until then can make things sticky. Then again, if you maintain a good relationship with the seller during the negotiation stage, this may be the time you're rewarded for it. The seller may agree either to repair any badly damaged walls or grant you a monetary credit at the closing.

Repairs and cleaning

Except for minor problems and anything specified in the purchase agreement, the seller must turn over the house to you in the same condition as when the contract was agreed upon. Usually, that means all systems work just as they did when you had the home inspected. Before the closing, you and your Realtor should do a walk-through to make sure the house is just as it was.

Homeowner warranties

Some sellers are willing to provide a warranty (either through themselves or through their Realtor) for all appliances, fixtures, heating, air conditioning, plumbing, and electrical systems, and even for the roof. Warranties are usually offered in a buyer's market as a marketing incentive. In addition, some companies offer warranties for a fee.

For new homes, the builder offers a warranty and, in fact, is required to stand by the work for a period of time. For resales of existing homes, there are no such laws. So if the warranty is offered and built into the price, that means that the seller has already purchased a plan. Make sure you understand the specific terms, since most are limited warranties. There are usually deductibles, like most insurance programs, and not everything is covered (for example, an aging furnace; such normal wear and tear through age is not covered).

CHAPTER 9

selecting a mortgage

IN THIS CHAPTER

- Understanding mortgages
- Choosing the right mortgage

This chapter contains explanations of the terms and sources of a mortgage, and descriptions of some of the fees you'll be charged. When the day finally comes to close on the deal, you'll be able to receive and endorse over to the seller the biggest cheque you've probably ever seen.

All about Mortgages

A mortgage is nothing more than a specific type of loan — a loan used to purchase a home. You legally own the home and you can live in the home, and you maintain it and make improvements to it. But in truth, your ownership is shared with the lender until many years later, when you pay off the loan. If you don't pay your mortgage, the lender can take legal ownership from you. At the *closing* (when you actually buy the house), you give the seller a down payment and the rest of the seller's money comes from your mortgage company.

The best down payment is at least 20 percent of the total cost of the house. That way, you don't have to pay for mortgage insurance.

Where to get a mortgage

You may be shocked to learn that there are an almost unlimited number of companies who want to lend you money. Because lenders rarely put up more than 80 percent of the cost of the house without insurance, they know that if worse comes to worst, they can always take back the house, sell it, and recoup their investment.

Remember, if a lender puts up more than 80 percent they will make you buy an insurance policy so their investment is still safe. Rarely does a house drop more than 20 percent in value, so 80 percent is a pretty safe investment.

Sources of mortgages

Many different types of institutions are eager to lend money to you to buy a home if they are reasonably assured you will be able to repay the loan. Some of the lenders are:

- **Banks:** The traditional source of mortgages, they still provide the majority of loans. And don't rule out online banks, which can offer great rates and a hassle-free application process.
- **Trust companies:** Also quite traditional, and sometimes, because many are small, local companies, they can provide one-on-one service.

- **Credit unions:** Because their services are available only to members, their loan rates and terms are often quite attractive.
- **Private lenders:** Because private lenders don't have to follow the same rules as large companies, sometimes the mortgage terms can be extremely attractive. And private lenders can be more flexible with borrowers who have poor credit ratings, or no credit history. Many private lenders sell the loan to another investor, often before all the paperwork is complete, so that they don't have to deal with the collection process.

  Finding a private lender is usually handled by a mortgage broker, although now many lenders are available through the Internet.

Finding a lender

When you're looking to borrow money, one of the best sources of information is your real estate agent. Most Realtors keep a list of banks, trust companies, and mortgage brokers who do business with the agency. Even if you have a particular banker or broker with whom you've done business before, you should still check with other lenders. Market conditions for mortgages constantly change and the field is highly competitive, so the lender with the best terms yesterday may not offer the best terms today. On the other hand, lenders like repeat customers and often offer "good customer" discounts. So you should allow the banker or broker with whom you've done business before to compete. You can only win by comparing rates and terms of several lenders.

Consider starting your search with the lenders who deal with your real estate agency. Call several lenders and mortgage brokers and find out what terms they're currently offering on mortgage loans (most will give you quotes over the phone).

As you learn more about the different terms and options for mortgages, you can compare the different lenders.

You may discover that several lenders are offering the same rates and terms. To choose the right one, answer these questions:

- ☐ **Have you had a positive experience with the lender/ broker previously?**
- ☐ **Has your realty company done business with the lender/ broker?** If so, were they satisfied with the company?
- ☐ **Do you know or can you get the names of anyone else who has done business with the lender/broker?** You can ask the lender/broker for references.
- ☐ **Does the deal being offered seem too good to be true or is it in line with the other lenders and brokers you checked with?** Deals that are too good to be true may have consequences that are not obvious, such as hidden fees or legal loopholes that could cost you more later on.
- ☐ **Does the lender/broker offer you the opportunity to be pre-qualified and/or pre-approved?** Pre-qualified means that the lender has reviewed your application and found no reason to disqualify you from borrowing. If you're pre-approved, you're also pre-qualified, but the lender also has evaluated how much you can borrow. In that case all that remains to get a mortgage is the lender's appraisal of the house.
- ☐ **Is the lender/broker willing to offer a mortgage if your credit is not perfect?** If your credit rating is less than clear, chances are you'll have to pay a higher interest rate or will have to make a larger down payment. Again, a mortgage broker might be able to help you deal with a credit problem before it prevents you from getting a mortgage.

❑ **Does the lender/broker seem to be knowledgeable about the loan programs?** If not, you may be able to get better terms with another lender.

❑ **Does the lender/broker take the time to explain the various loan programs and features?** If not, you may not know all the relevant terms and conditions.

❑ **How many lenders does the mortgage broker work with?** If only a few, you may not be getting the best terms. On the other hand, a broker has a greater incentive than a bank to find you a mortgage: she gets paid only if the mortgage is placed — a bank loans officer gets paid no matter what.

❑ **Will the lender/broker come to you or will you have to go there?** You shouldn't have to pay any extra for the convenience of the broker coming to your home or office to sign all the papers.

❑ **Do you feel that the lender/broker is trustworthy?**

❑ **Do you and the lender/broker have a good rapport?** You enter into a trust relationship with a lender/broker. That can help you as you try to understand all the complicated terms and are evaluating different options.

Using the Internet

A growing number of sites are devoted to offering home mortgages. Websites are advertised on TV and the radio; in newspapers; and as banners, the advertisements that run across the tops of pages on other websites.

By all means check out what's online. Most of the lenders are legitimate and either are online mortgage brokers or represent a particular lender. Some of the sites act like e-bots, which are programs that search the Web to find the best deal for you.

Never (repeat, *never*) sign up or pay anything to any organization until you thoroughly check it out. Also, mortgages are legal documents with lots of fine print, about which you should be very wary. So, especially when it comes to online mortgage services, be certain to read all the fine print.

Before you sign up with any online lender (or any offline lender), compare *all* the terms being offered.

Choosing the Right Mortgage

You must know all the terms and conditions involved to select the best mortgage for you. You need to know about:

- Interest rates
- Length of the loan
- Fees

Interest rates

Clearly, all things being equal, the lower the interest rate, the better the mortgage is for you. But there are variables when it comes to understanding interest rates.

- **Fixed-rate loans:** With a *fixed-rate mortgage* you pay the same amount of interest each month for the entire life of the loan.
- **Adjustable-rate loans:** With a *variable-rate mortgage* (VRM), the interest rate changes periodically. How often and how much the rate changes depends on the type of loan.
- **Multi-rate loans:** With a *multi-rate loan*, the mortgage amount is divided into different segments, each with its own term, interest rate, payment schedule, and so on.

How much the interest rate on VRMs can change and why they change is different for different loans. And their repayment schedules can be flexible. For instance, a typical VRM might require you to make the same payment every month, yet apply more or less to the principal depending on whether the interest rate has risen or fallen.

Table 9-1 condenses the information of various types of mortgages.

Table 9-1: Types of Mortgage Interest Rates

Fixed-Rate Mortgages	The interest rate remains constant for the term of the loan.
Variable-Rate Mortgages	Interest rates are fixed for a specified period — then adjusted with prescribed limits on the amount it can adjust.
Multi-Rate Mortgages	Interest rates are a combination of variable and fixed.

The decision about which mortgage is best for you depends not only on interest rates, but on other variables as well. Some guidelines for selecting a fixed-rate or variable-rate mortgage are:

- If you plan to move from your home or refinance the mortgage within five years or so, the VRM is probably better for you because you usually pay a lower rate in the initial period of a VRM. If you're convinced interest rates are going to decline, a VRM is also a good choice.
- Conversely, if you plan to stay in this home for the rest of your life and interest rates have hit an all-time low (they really can't go much lower), a fixed rate is probably better. But keep in mind that people stay in their home an average of five to seven years.

- If you are confident that your income will rise steadily over the years and want to borrow more than a fixed-rate mortgage allows (because, for example, you want more house now), a VRM is better since the initial interest rate is lower. If you get an inkling that interest rates are on the rise, you can always lock in the rate.

- If you don't have the stomach to handle changing interest rates, especially if you're already pushed to your limit as to how much you can afford, choose a fixed rate.

Closed versus open mortgages

Which type of mortgage you get in part relies on what repayment options you want. A *closed* mortgage is one that you can't prepay (pay off before the maturity date) or refinance or renegotiate in any way before maturity, without being hit with a prepayment penalty — usually three months of mortgage payments or the interest rate differential, whichever is greater. An *open* mortgage allows you to prepay at any time, in part or in full.

Which is right for you? That depends. If interest rates are high and/or you plan on moving in the near future, an open mortgage will give you the flexibility you might need. Remember, though, that the interest rate is usually higher for these kinds of loans, and it is very hard to find an open mortgage for a term longer than six months to one year. A closed mortgage could be more suitable if interest rates are low and you're confident that you're not going to move in the near future.

The length of the loan

Amortization periods (the time it takes for you to pay off the mortgage in total) can vary. But typically, you can choose to pay off your mortgage over either 15 years or 25 years. The amortization period you choose affects how much your monthly mortgage payment is and the interest rate you get on your loan.

- **25-year mortgage:** This is the most common mortgage length and means that your loan is amortized over 25 years. The total amount of interest you pay over 25 years at 5 percent interest equals about 75 percent of the amount of the loan itself. *Amortized* means the repayment of a loan with payments calculated so that the loan is paid off at the end of the loan period.
- **15-year mortgage:** The monthly payments for a 15-year mortgage are generally about 25 percent higher than the payments for a 25-year mortgage, which makes sense because you pay the whole loan amount in less time. The total amount of interest you pay over 15 years at 5 percent interest equals about 40 percent of the amount you originally borrow.

Generally, the interest rate for a 15-year mortgage is a little lower than for a 25-year loan, usually about .25 percent.

Consider the following when deciding between a 15- and 25-year mortgage:

- If the monthly payments for a 15-year term loan will strain your budget, select the 25-year term.
- If you plan to move or refinance within five to seven years and can afford the higher payment, select the 15-year term. You will have paid off more of the loan at a lower interest rate.
- If you plan to stay in this house for the entire loan period, you have a low (and fixed) interest rate, can afford the higher monthly payments, and are anxious to own your home free and clear as soon as possible, select a 15-year mortgage.

Keep in mind that you can usually pay down the loan faster than the term specified. In this case, the monthly payment is the *minimum* you must pay — and on an open mortgage, at least, there is generally no maximum (except that you may not be allowed to repay the entire loan in the first few months). Even for most closed mortgages, you can pay as much as 15 percent of the loan amount (principal) on the anniversary date of the mortgage, and you can also pay up to 15 percent extra on your monthly payments if you have some spare cash. So if you have extra funds in any month, or receive a bonus that you wish to put toward your house, you can always pay a lump sum to your lender, thereby reducing the principal. (Make sure that you specify that you want the extra amount applied to the principal and not to the next month's payment.)

Another good way to pay off your mortgage faster is to pay more frequently. Instead of once a month, consider making mortgage payments every two weeks. (That can be really convenient if you, like many Canadian workers, get a fortnightly paycheque.) A mortgage payment every two weeks dramatically reduces the time it takes to pay off the loan.

Paying off your home is not always the best use of additional funds. You may be able to get a better return by investing those funds somewhere else, especially if the other investment is a tax-deferred retirement account.

Other fees

Most lenders require you to pay several fees. Some fees are negotiable and some are required. Some fees are built in to the normal charges you pay, and some you pay at the closing. Typical fees include:

- **Application and processing fees:** Most lenders charge about $150 to process your mortgage application. This fee may be waived or eliminated, especially if the lender is actively looking for borrowers. The process fee is negotiable because it is really just the lender's cost of doing business.
- **Appraisal fee:** Before determining whether to lend you the money to buy your home, the lender must be assured that if you don't pay the loan back, the lender can get her money back. So the lender needs to know how much the house is worth and hires an appraiser to inspect and evaluate the property. The fee for this appraisal is often passed on to you and runs at about $250 or so. You may be able to get this fee waived since it really is nothing more than the lender's cost of insuring that she can get the money back if you default. On high-ratio mortgages insured by CMHC or Genworth, there are no appraisal fees.
- **Document fees:** These fees are for all sorts of miscellaneous expenses on the lender's part. They are almost all negotiable because they are part of the normal cost of doing business.
- **Lock-in fee:** You may be concerned that interest rates will go up before you actually close on your home. Some lenders charge you a fee to "lock in" the rate at the time of your application so that if rates go up, you are protected. This fee is negotiable since many lenders will agree to lock in the rate within 60 days of the closing.
- **CMHC charge:** If you arranged a CMHC-approved mortgage, you will have to pay insurance premiums of between 0.5 percent and 6 percent of the purchase price.

CHAPTER 10

making it yours

IN THIS CHAPTER

- Purchase agreements
- Ownership
- The closing and settlement

Throughout the home-buying process, keep in mind that buying a house means entering the world of contract law. And as with any contract, you must pay close attention to the fine print and look for loopholes in your purchase agreement. At the *closing* (when the money is exchanged and the property is legally transferred to you), you sign so many forms your hand may get sore.

When in doubt, consult a lawyer or notary! When buying a home, if there is anything you don't understand about a form you must sign, ask a professional about it — your Realtor or a lawyer.

If the province in which you are buying property does not require that a lawyer be involved in the buying process and you are uncertain about any of the language, forms, or processes, or you are not sure of your rights, *hire an expert in real estate law.*

Real estate agents ultimately work for the buyer or the seller (or both under dual agency). Review Chapter 6 for the ins and outs of who your Realtor works for.

The Offer to Purchase

The opening round in your legal manoeuvres with the seller is the *offer to purchase* — a legal document which states that you agree to buy the seller's house, dependent on certain conditions. Your Realtor represents you in negotiations with the seller. The purchase agreement is a flexible legal agreement with many uses. Through this document you:

- Make your initial offer to the seller, specifying the price you will pay.
- Itemize what you want included in the sale.
- Specify what must happen and when for the deal to go through (the *contingencies* or *conditions*), including how much you're borrowing to pay for the house and when the closing will take place.
- List the dates by which all the contingencies will be removed, such as how many days for a lawyer review or home inspection.
- List the amount of your deposit or *earnest money*, which accompanies the offer and is deposited in an escrow account set up on your behalf by the Realtor (you may be able to use a personal cheque but be prepared to get a bank draft). It's usually 5 percent or so of the offer price.

- Receive any counter-offers from the seller.
- Make your counter-counter-offers (and receive counter-counter-counter-offers, and so on).
- Reach a final agreement with the seller.

The offer is signed and initialled where changes are made to the original offer that reflect new offers and agreements. When the negotiations are complete and all the terms are agreed upon, you will be given a copy of the final accepted offer with all the required initials and signatures in place.

Review your offer:

Check that the address of the property and legal description are written correctly. Make sure that your offer

- ❑ Lists any items you want included in the purchase that are not built in or attached, including any personal property (such as free-standing appliances, furnishings, window treatments, and so on).
- ❑ Lists any expenses you want the sellers to pay on your behalf (homeowner's dues, home warranties, professional carpet cleaning, and so on).
- ❑ Lists any repairs that must be made before the closing, or any credits for itemized damages.
- ❑ Make sure that the conditions of the sale aren't too restrictive. (For example, you don't want to be limited to just 30 days before closing unless you already have a mortgage arranged or know for sure that the specified time is sufficient.)

The agreement of purchase and sale is a legal document. If you have any concerns about it, you might wish to consult your lawyer before signing.

Ownership

If you have a mortgage on your property, you (and any partners, including your spouse) own it in conjunction with the lending institution. When you pay off your mortgage, you get full title. If you stop paying your mortgage, the lender can *foreclose* on the property and take it from you. If you sell your property, you incur either a gain or a loss on the sale. Your property is transferable by sale or foreclosure, and in the event of your death, the property and its debts, as part of your estate, pass to your heirs. (Insurance is available to pay off mortgages upon death.)

The *equity* in a property is its *market value* minus the amount owed on it.

Knowing how much equity you have in your property is critical for a number of reasons:

- The equity in your home counts as an asset when you apply for credit.
- If there is a legal judgment against you, the equity in your home is available to your creditors.
- If you need money for any reason, you may be able to borrow against the equity in your home (hence the term *home equity loan*).

You can co-own property in several different ways. The type of co-ownership determines how you handle the gain on the sale of the property, and how the property is passed on to your heirs after your death. It's important to know these types before you buy so that you specify the form of co-ownership correctly from the beginning. If you need to change the ownership, you may have to pay lawyer's fees, recording fees, or even taxes.

You and your partner(s) usually choose from the following forms of ownership:

- Joint tenancy
- Tenancy in common

When speaking with your lawyer or notary about buying a property, ask about the best form of ownership for you. Usually when buying a first home, this process is not very complicated.

Joint tenancy

With joint tenancy, both (all) partners own equal shares in the property. When one partner dies, the ownership is automatically transferred to the surviving partner(s). All partners have an undivided interest.

Tenancy in common

With tenancy in common, each partner owns an undivided interest in the total property but there is no automatic right of survivorship. Each partner may sell or will his or her portion to another person, whether or not the other partner approves.

If a deed does not specify joint tenancy or if the partners are not married, the law almost always presumes that ownership is tenancy in common.

The Closing

Between the time your offer is accepted and the time you take possession of your new home, a lot of work has to be done — much of it best left to your lawyer/notary. Here are some of the steps in the often-complicated process of closing a real estate transaction:

The survey

Usually, you'll have to make sure an up-to-date survey is available for the property you want to buy — most lenders require it to show exactly what they are lending you money for. Your lawyer, in preparing the mortgage documents, uses the survey to help her provide a legal opinion about encroachments, easements, liens, and other matters that might hinder your ownership of the property.

If a survey isn't available, one option is title insurance, which can be used to protect your mortgage in case of title problems. Your lawyer or Realtor can provide more information about title insurance, which usually costs between $150 and $250.

The title search

Your lawyer searches the title to the property you want to buy. Among other things, she makes sure that there are no easements or encroachments on the property, and, most important, that the seller actually owns it so that you can buy it without any legal problems.

The statement of adjustment

When your lawyer has added it all up, reviewed the agreement of purchase and sale, and finalized the mortgage documents, she will let you know exactly what you have to pay, and for what, before closing the deal. This is more complicated than it sounds, as buying a home involves a whole lot of disparate fees, taxes, and other charges.

If *anything* does not look right, or if you do not understand something, ask about it.

The following list explains some of the more important charges on a statement of adjustment:

- **Gross Amount Due from Borrower:** This is the agreed-upon sales price plus any charges for which you are responsible, such as mortgage origination fees, dues, and prepaid mortgage interest for the month. It also includes money you need to pay to your lender for any annual property taxes and homeowner's insurance. You usually have to prepay an entire year's insurance premium and a pro-rated amount of the annual property taxes.

- **Amounts Paid By or On Behalf of Borrower:** This is the amount you paid as earnest money (your deposit), the total from your loan(s), and any adjustments for items that the seller is responsible for paying but hasn't yet paid (taxes and dues to the current date).

- **Gross Amount Due to Sellers and Reductions in Amount Due to Sellers:** This reflects the amounts paid by the sellers and due them. These amounts include credits for any money the sellers paid in advance for which you are responsible (prepaid property taxes, dues, and so on) and the commission to the Realtor.

- **Land Transfer Tax:** In some provinces and/or municipalities, you have to pay a tax for purchasing a home, and it can run into the thousands.

- **Goods and Services Tax (GST) or Harmonised Sales Tax (HST):** If you're buying a resale home, you don't have to pay the dreaded GST/HST; if you're buying a new home, you do — but the rate is reduced from 5 percent to 3.5 percent on houses worth less than $350,000, thanks to the GST/HST New Housing Rebate. The rebate is gradually reduced for homes valued from $350,000 to the maximum value of $450,000.

• **Legal fees:** What your lawyer gets for doing all this work. Typical fees are $650 and up.

Although most of the time these fees are reasonable, sometimes they can get a bit outrageous, as when your lawyer charges you hundreds of dollars for making copies of documents. Absolutely raise the issue and try to get the amount reduced.

The big cheque

This is the exciting moment — when you finally pay for your new home. Your lender will deposit the agreed-upon mortgage amount into an account held by your lawyer; you give your lawyer a certified cheque for the balance (down payment, outstanding fees and adjustments — all that stuff). Then the seller is paid, the land is registered in your name, and your lawyer gives you the deed — and you get the keys to your new home!

And Finally, It's Yours

Buying a home can be one of the most joyful experiences in your life. When the last document is signed, you can lean back in your chair, try to shake the numbness out of your writing hand, and receive the keys to your new home. Your next step will be opening the front door of your new home and stepping inside. Just imagine the smile on your face!

final review

Use this Final Review to practise what you've learned in this book and to build your confidence in doing the job right the first time. After you work through the review questions and the problem-solving scenario, you'll be well on your way to achieving your goal of buying your first home.

Q&A

1. What are the two main differences between a condominium and a single-family home?

    1. _____

       _____

    2. _____

       _____

2. Name five key players in the home-buying process and explain how they each get paid.

1. _____

_____

_____

2. _____

_____

_____

3. _____

_____

_____

4. _____

_____

_____

5. _____

_____

_____

3. Before making an offer to buy a home, you should have answers to all but which of these questions:

   a. What have comparable homes in the area sold for?
   b. How long was the home on the market?
   c. How much did the sellers pay for the home?
   d. At what price was the home initially listed?

4. True or false: Light fixtures and appliances that are physically attached to the house are always included with the purchase.

5. Most lenders require that the payment on your mortgage, including the amount they hold in escrow for your home-owner's insurance and property taxes, not exceed what percent of your gross monthly income?

    a. 26%
    b. 28%
    c. 32%
    d. 35%

6. What is leveraging?

_____
_____
_____
_____
_____
_____
_____

Scenario

You want to purchase a home for $200,000 and have $25,000 available for your down payment and fees. Your income is enough to support a loan of $180,000, which is 90 percent of the purchase price. But if you borrow that much, the lender will require you to pay mortgage insurance, which you would prefer not to buy. What can you do?

_____
_____
_____
_____
_____

Answers

Q&A Answers

1. Condos are not actual types of buildings but a form of ownership. With a condo, you share ownership of the entire condominium complex, not just your home.
2. Realtor: usually gets paid by the seller from proceeds of the sale; Lawyer or notary: gets paid by you directly; Home inspector: gets paid by you directly; Insurance agent: gets paid by you either directly or through escrow; Mortgage broker: gets paid by the lender. (
3. c. (Of course you're curious, but this doesn't really have an effect on the current price.)
4. False. Usually, but not always.
5. b
6. Leveraging is an investing tool by which a little bit of money invested in a large investment can produce large gains, much like a lever enables you to move heavy objects.

Scenario Answer

Get a first mortgage of $150,000 (75 percent of the price) and a second mortgage of $10,000 (5 percent). As an alternative, you may be able to borrow the $10,000 from your family.

resource centre

Internet

Any number of websites offer to find you the best house, the best Realtor, and the best mortgage rate. Of course, no site can be all things to all homebuyers, but going online can certainly help you explore the possibilities as you buy your first home. You should find the sites listed below especially helpful. Check out these sites for more information about home buying and more:

Websites like **Canoe Money,** accessible at canoe.ca, and **RBC Royal Bank's Mortgage Centre,** at rbcroyalbank.com, link you to calculators that tell you how much home you can afford and calculate mortgage rates and payments. Both sites also offer plenty of information and tips for homebuyers, home sellers, and home renters.

MLS Online, at realtor.ca, is the official gateway to Canadian MLS listings. If a home is listed for sale in Canada through a member of the Canadian Real Estate Association (whose own site is at crea.ca), this is the best place to find it.

ForSaleByOwner and PropertySold, at forsalebyowner.ca and propertysold.ca, are geared to sellers who want to do it themselves. But the latter also offers additional information about everything from getting the lowest price on a mortgage to renos that sell.

If you want to check your credit rating before buying a home, you can find more information about **Equifax Canada,** one of the main credit bureaus in the country, at its site, www.equifax.ca.

You can also check out your rating with **Trans Union Canada** (transunion.ca). Reach them at 1-800-663-9980 or (for Quebec residents) 1-877-713-3393 or 514-335-0374.

notes

notes

notes

_____
_____
_____
_____
_____
_____
_____
_____
_____
_____
_____
_____
_____
_____
_____
_____
_____
_____
_____
_____
_____
_____
_____
_____
_____
_____

notes